The Linux Operating System

A guide for beginners

January 2025

Charles Barclay

Table of Contents

Introduction

Welcome to the exciting world of Linux! This book is your friendly, beginner's guide to understanding and using the Linux operating system. Whether you're a complete novice to the world of computers or an experienced user looking to expand your skillset, this guide will provide you with a solid foundation in Linux.

What exactly is Linux, you might ask? Well, in simple terms, Linux is a powerful and versatile operating system, much like Windows or macOS. However, unlike those commercial systems, Linux is open-source. This means its underlying code is freely available to anyone who wants to view, modify, and distribute it. This openness has fostered a vibrant community of developers and users who contribute to its ongoing development, making Linux a highly customizable and adaptable system. It is important to remember that the term "Linux" is often used to refer to the entire operating system, but technically, it refers specifically to the Linux kernel.

The kernel is the heart of the operating system, the core component that manages the computer's hardware resources and enables communication between software and hardware. However, a kernel alone is not enough to provide a fully functional operating system. To achieve this, the Linux kernel is typically combined with a variety of other software components, such as a shell, core utilities, and libraries, to create what is known as a "Linux distribution."

Linux distributions, often referred to as "distros," are essentially different flavors of Linux. Some of the most popular distributions include Ubuntu, Fedora, Debian, and Linux Mint. Each distro has its own unique set of features, user interfaces, and package management systems. Choosing the right distro for you will depend on your specific needs and preferences. For example, Ubuntu is often recommended for beginners due to its user-friendly interface and extensive software repositories. Fedora, on the other hand, is known for its cutting-edge technology and is a popular choice among developers. And Debian is renowned for its stability and commitment to free software principles.

One of the key advantages of Linux is its flexibility. It can run on a wide range of devices, from supercomputers and servers to desktops, laptops, and even smartphones. In fact, the Android operating system, which powers the majority of smartphones worldwide, is based on the Linux kernel. This versatility makes Linux a valuable skill to have in today's tech-driven world. Linux also has the advantage of being much more resistant to malware than alternative operating systems such as Microsoft Windows.

Another compelling reason to learn Linux is its command-line interface (CLI). While graphical user interfaces (GUIs) are great for everyday tasks, the command line offers a level of control and efficiency that is unmatched. By typing commands into the terminal, you can interact directly with the operating system, perform complex operations, automate tasks, and troubleshoot issues with precision. Mastering the command line can significantly boost your productivity and give you a deeper understanding of how Linux works.

Throughout this book, we will explore the fundamentals of Linux, starting with the basics of navigating the filesystem and using the command line. We will then delve into essential command-line tools, file and directory management, user and group administration, file permissions, and process management. We will also cover system monitoring, package management, shell scripting, networking, remote access, text editors, and system administration basics. We'll even touch upon installing and configuring a web server, an introduction to databases, and security best practices.

Each chapter is designed to build upon the previous one, gradually introducing new concepts and techniques. We will use clear and concise language, avoiding technical jargon whenever possible. You'll find practical examples and hands-on exercises to help you reinforce your learning and gain confidence in using Linux. No prior experience with Linux or programming is required. We will start from the very beginning, assuming you have basic computer literacy. However, a willingness to learn and experiment is essential.

Linux might seem daunting at first, especially if you're accustomed to graphical operating systems. But don't worry; we will guide you every step of the way. Remember, learning a new operating system is like learning a new language. It takes time, practice, and patience. But once you become proficient, you'll be amazed at what you can accomplish.

One of the best things about Linux is its active and supportive community. There are countless online forums, communities, and resources available to help you along your journey. If you ever get stuck or have a question, don't hesitate to reach out to the community for assistance. You'll find that Linux users are generally passionate and eager to help newcomers.

Before we dive into the technical details, let's briefly address the history of Linux. It all started in 1991 when a Finnish student named Linus Torvalds began working on a new operating system kernel as a hobby project. He shared his work with the world, inviting others to contribute and improve upon it. This collaborative effort quickly gained momentum, and soon, developers from all over the globe were contributing to the project.

Over the years, Linux has evolved into a mature and robust operating system, powering a significant portion of the internet's infrastructure, including web servers, cloud computing platforms, and scientific research facilities. Its open-source nature has made it a favorite among developers, system administrators, and tech enthusiasts.

In this book, we will primarily focus on using Linux in a desktop environment. However, it's important to note that Linux is also widely used in server environments. In fact, many websites and online services that you use every day are likely running on Linux servers. Learning Linux can open up a world of opportunities, whether you're interested in web development, system administration, cybersecurity, or simply want to become a more proficient computer user.

As you progress through this book, keep in mind that Linux is a vast and constantly evolving ecosystem. There's always something new to learn, and the possibilities are virtually endless. Don't be afraid to explore, experiment, and try new things. The more you use Linux, the more comfortable and confident you'll become.

One common misconception about Linux is that it's only for programmers or "hackers." While it's true that Linux is popular among technical users, it's also perfectly suitable for everyday users who simply want a reliable, secure, and customizable operating system. With user-friendly distributions like Ubuntu and Linux Mint, anyone can install and use Linux without needing to know how to code.

Another myth is that Linux is difficult to install. In the past, this might have been true, but nowadays, most Linux distributions offer easy-to-use graphical installers that guide you through the process step-by-step. In many cases, installing Linux is just as straightforward as installing Windows or macOS.

Some people also worry about software compatibility. While it's true that not all Windows or macOS applications have direct Linux equivalents, there are often open-source alternatives available that provide similar functionality. For example, instead of Microsoft Office, you can use LibreOffice, a free and open-source office suite. And for web browsing, you can use Firefox or Chromium, the open-source version of Google Chrome.

Moreover, many popular applications, such as the Firefox web browser, the VLC media player, and the GIMP image editor, are cross-platform and have native Linux versions. Additionally, there's a compatibility layer called Wine that allows you to run many Windows applications directly on Linux.

In terms of hardware support, Linux has come a long way. Most modern hardware components are automatically detected and configured during installation. However, it's always a good idea to check the hardware compatibility list of your chosen distribution before installing it, especially if you have older or less common hardware.

One of the key strengths of Linux is its security. Due to its open-source nature, any vulnerabilities are quickly identified and patched by the community. Additionally, Linux's user and permission model makes it more difficult for malware to gain root access and compromise the system. While no operating system is completely immune to security threats, Linux is generally considered more secure than Windows, especially when best practices are followed.

Another advantage of Linux is its stability. Linux systems are known for their reliability and uptime. It's not uncommon for Linux servers to run for months or even years without requiring a reboot. This stability makes Linux an excellent choice for mission-critical applications and services.

Furthermore, Linux is highly customizable. You can change almost every aspect of the system, from the desktop environment and window manager to the default applications and system settings. This level of customization allows you to tailor your Linux system to your exact needs and preferences.

Linux also offers a wide range of development tools and programming languages. Whether you're interested in web development, mobile app development, or scientific computing, you'll find that Linux provides a powerful and flexible environment for your projects.

In addition to its technical merits, Linux also embodies a philosophy of openness, collaboration, and community. By using and contributing to Linux, you become part of a global movement that values user freedom, knowledge sharing, and technological innovation.

As we embark on this journey together, remember that learning Linux is not just about mastering a new operating system; it's about embracing a new way of thinking about technology. It's about taking control of your computing experience and becoming an active participant in the digital world.

So, whether you're a student, a professional, or simply a curious individual, this book will provide you with the knowledge and skills you need to start using Linux with confidence. Get ready to unlock the power and potential of the Linux operating system. Let's begin!

CHAPTER ONE: Getting Started with Linux

This chapter will guide you through the initial steps of getting started with Linux. We'll cover the basics of choosing a distribution, installing it on your computer, and familiarizing yourself with the desktop environment. By the end of this chapter, you'll have a working Linux system and be ready to explore its features. The first thing you need to do when starting with Linux is to choose a distribution, often called a "distro." As we learned in the introduction, a distribution is a complete operating system built on top of the Linux kernel, bundled with various software packages, a desktop environment, and a package manager. There are hundreds of Linux distributions available, each with its own unique features and target audience.

For beginners, it's generally recommended to start with a user-friendly distribution that offers a smooth out-of-the-box experience. Some popular choices for newcomers include Ubuntu, Linux Mint, and Fedora. Ubuntu is known for its ease of use, extensive software repositories, and large community support. Linux Mint, based on Ubuntu, provides a more traditional desktop experience and is often praised for its simplicity and stability. Fedora, on the other hand, is a community-driven distribution that focuses on free and open-source software and is known for incorporating the latest technologies. Other beginner-friendly distributions include Pop!_OS, elementary OS, and Zorin OS. Each of these distros offers a straightforward installation process, a user-friendly interface, and a wide range of pre-installed applications.

Once you've chosen a distribution, you'll need to download its installation image, usually in the form of an ISO file. An ISO file is a disk image that contains all the necessary files to install the operating system. You can download the ISO file from the official website of your chosen distribution. After downloading the ISO file, you'll need to create a bootable USB drive or DVD. This will allow you to boot your computer from the installation media and start the installation process. There are several tools available for creating bootable USB drives, such as Rufus, Etcher, and UNetbootin. These tools are available for Windows, macOS, and Linux.

The process of creating a bootable USB drive typically involves selecting the ISO file, choosing the target USB drive, and starting the writing process. It's important to note that this process will erase all existing data on the USB drive, so make sure to back up any important files beforehand. Once the bootable USB drive is ready, you'll need to configure your computer to boot from it. This usually involves entering the BIOS or UEFI settings during startup and changing the boot order to prioritize the USB drive. The exact steps for accessing the BIOS or UEFI settings vary depending on your computer's make and model.

With the boot order configured, you can now insert the bootable USB drive and restart your computer. If everything is set up correctly, your computer should boot from the USB drive and launch the Linux installer. Most Linux installers offer a graphical interface that guides you through the installation process step-by-step. You'll typically be asked to choose your language, time zone, keyboard layout, and disk partitioning options. Disk partitioning is the process of dividing your hard drive into one or more sections, called partitions. This allows you to allocate space for the Linux installation and, optionally, create separate partitions for your personal files.

If you're new to Linux, it's generally recommended to choose the automatic partitioning option, which will automatically create the necessary partitions for you. However, if you have specific requirements or want more control over the partitioning process, you can choose the manual partitioning option. During the installation, you'll also be prompted to create a user account. This will be your primary account for logging into the system and performing administrative tasks. You'll need to choose a username and a strong password. It's important to choose a password that is difficult to guess but easy for you to remember.

After the installation is complete, you'll be prompted to remove the installation media and reboot your computer. Once your computer restarts, it should boot into your newly installed Linux system. You'll be greeted with the login screen, where you can enter your username and password to log in. Upon logging in, you'll be presented with the desktop environment. The desktop environment is the graphical interface that allows you to interact with the operating system using windows, icons, and menus. Different distributions use different desktop environments, each with its own look and feel.

Some popular desktop environments include GNOME, KDE Plasma, Xfce, and Cinnamon. GNOME is the default desktop environment for many distributions, including Ubuntu and Fedora. It features a modern and minimalist design with a focus on simplicity and ease of use. KDE Plasma is another popular choice, known for its flexibility and customization options. Xfce is a lightweight desktop environment that is ideal for older or less powerful computers. Cinnamon, developed by the Linux Mint team, offers a traditional desktop layout with a familiar taskbar and start menu.

Once you're logged into the desktop environment, take some time to explore its features. You'll typically find a taskbar or panel at the bottom or top of the screen, which contains icons for launching applications, accessing system settings, and managing open windows. There's usually a start menu or application launcher that allows you to browse and launch installed applications. Most desktop environments also provide a system tray or notification area, where you can find icons for system functions like network connectivity, volume control, and power management. You can customize the appearance and behavior of the desktop environment to suit your preferences.

You can change the wallpaper, themes, icons, and fonts. You can also add or remove panels, widgets, and applets. Experiment with different settings and find a configuration that you find comfortable and visually appealing. One of the first things you might want to do after installing Linux is to connect to the internet.

Most Linux distributions automatically detect and configure network connections during installation. If you're using a wired connection, you should be connected to the internet automatically. If you're using a wireless connection, you'll need to select your Wi-Fi network and enter the password.

Once you're connected to the internet, you can start exploring the vast world of Linux software. Linux distributions use package managers to manage the installation, updating, and removal of software packages. A package manager is a tool that automates the process of installing, updating, and removing software. It also handles dependencies, which are other software packages that a particular program requires to function correctly. Different distributions use different package managers. For example, Ubuntu and Debian-based distributions use APT (Advanced Package Tool), while Fedora and Red Hat-based distributions use DNF (Dandified YUM).

To install software using the package manager, you can use either the command-line interface or a graphical front-end. For example, in Ubuntu, you can use the Software Center, which provides a user-friendly interface for browsing and installing applications. Alternatively, you can use the apt command in the terminal to install software. For example, to install the VLC media player, you would open the terminal and type

```
sudo apt install vlc
```

. The sudo command is used to execute commands with administrative privileges, which are required for installing software.

Updating your system is an important part of maintaining a secure and stable Linux installation. Most distributions provide a graphical tool for managing updates, such as the Software Updater in Ubuntu. You can also update your system using the command-line interface. For example, to update all installed packages in Ubuntu, you would open the terminal and type

```
sudo apt update && sudo apt upgrade
```

. The

```
sudo apt update
```

command updates the package lists, while

```
sudo apt upgrade
```

upgrades the installed packages to their latest versions.

As you become more comfortable with Linux, you'll likely want to explore the command-line interface in more depth. The command line, also known as the terminal or shell, is a powerful tool that allows you to interact with the operating system by typing commands. While the graphical interface is great for everyday tasks, the command line offers a level of control and efficiency that is unmatched. To open the terminal, you can usually press Ctrl+Alt+T or search for "terminal" in the application menu. Once the terminal is open, you'll be presented with a prompt, which typically displays your username, the hostname of your computer, and the current working directory.

The command line might seem intimidating at first, but with practice, you'll find that it's a powerful and efficient way to interact with your Linux system. We'll cover the basics of navigating the command line in the next chapter. In this chapter, we covered the initial steps of getting started with Linux. We discussed how to choose a distribution, download the installation image, create a bootable USB drive, install the operating system, and familiarize yourself with the desktop environment. We also touched upon connecting to the internet, installing software using the package manager, updating the system, and briefly introduced the command-line interface.

With your newly installed Linux system, you're now ready to embark on a journey of exploration and discovery. In the following chapters, we'll delve deeper into the various aspects of Linux, starting with understanding the Linux filesystem.

Remember, learning a new operating system takes time and practice. Don't be afraid to experiment, try new things, and make mistakes. The Linux community is vast and supportive, so don't hesitate to seek help if you encounter any issues. There are countless online forums, communities, and resources available to assist you along the way.

As you continue to use Linux, you'll discover its power, flexibility, and versatility. You'll learn how to customize your system, automate tasks, and troubleshoot issues. You'll gain a deeper understanding of how operating systems work and how to harness their full potential. Whether you're a student, a professional, or simply a curious individual, learning Linux is a valuable skill that can open up a world of opportunities. It's a journey that requires patience, persistence, and a willingness to learn. But with each step, you'll gain confidence and proficiency, unlocking the full potential of this remarkable operating system.

CHAPTER TWO: Understanding the Linux Filesystem

In this chapter, we will explore the structure and organization of the Linux filesystem. The filesystem is a crucial component of any operating system, as it determines how data is stored and accessed on your computer. Unlike some other operating systems, Linux has a unified filesystem hierarchy, which means that all files and directories are organized under a single root directory. This hierarchical structure makes it easy to navigate and manage files, regardless of their physical location on your storage devices. To better understand the Linux filesystem, let's start by examining its core principles.

At the very top of the Linux filesystem hierarchy is the root directory, represented by a forward slash (/). This is the starting point of the entire filesystem. Every other file and directory on your system is located under the root directory, either directly or indirectly. Think of it like the trunk of a tree, with all other directories branching out from it. One of the fundamental concepts in Linux is that everything is treated as a file. This includes not only regular files like documents, images, and videos but also directories, devices, and even processes.

This unified approach simplifies many operations and makes it easier to manage different aspects of the system. Within the root directory, you'll find several important subdirectories that serve specific purposes. For example, the /bin directory contains essential command-line utilities that are required for the system to function properly. These utilities are available to all users and include commands like ls, cp, and mv, which we'll explore in later chapters. The /boot directory holds the files needed to boot the operating system, including the Linux kernel, the initial RAM disk, and the bootloader.

The /dev directory contains device files, which represent physical devices such as hard drives, printers, and input devices. These files allow the operating system to interact with the hardware. In Linux, devices are treated as special files, which can be read from or written to, just like regular files. The /etc directory is where system-wide configuration files are stored. These files control various aspects of the operating system's behavior, such as network settings, user accounts, and startup scripts. Modifying these files requires administrative privileges, as they can affect the entire system.

The /home directory is where user home directories are located. Each user on the system typically has their own subdirectory within /home, where they can store their personal files, documents, and settings. For example, if your username is "john," your home directory would likely be /home/john. This separation of user data from system files helps maintain security and organization. The /lib directory contains shared libraries that are used by programs throughout the system. These libraries contain code that can be used by multiple programs, reducing redundancy and improving efficiency.

The /media directory is used for mounting removable media, such as USB drives and CDs. When you insert a removable device, the operating system automatically creates a subdirectory under /media and mounts the device there, making its contents accessible. The /mnt directory serves a similar purpose but is typically used for temporarily mounting filesystems, such as network shares. The /opt directory is reserved for optional software packages that are not part of the core system. These packages are often installed from third-party sources and are self-contained within their own subdirectories under /opt.

The /proc directory is a virtual filesystem that provides information about running processes and kernel parameters. It doesn't contain actual files stored on disk but rather dynamically generated data that reflects the current state of the system. The /root directory is the home directory for the root user, the superuser account that has administrative privileges over the entire system. It's separate from the regular user home directories in /home for security reasons. The /sbin directory contains system binaries, which are essential commands used for system administration tasks.

These commands are typically only accessible to the root user. The /srv directory is used for storing data related to services provided by the system, such as web server files or FTP directories. The /tmp directory is used for temporary files that are created by various programs. These files are usually deleted automatically when the system reboots or when they are no longer needed. The /usr directory is a large and important part of the filesystem that contains a hierarchy of subdirectories for user-related programs, libraries, documentation, and other data.

It's designed to be read-only, except during software installation or updates. Within /usr, you'll find subdirectories like /usr/bin, which contains user commands; /usr/sbin, which contains system administration commands; /usr/lib, which contains libraries; and /usr/share, which contains architecture-independent data. The /var directory contains variable data, which is data that changes frequently during normal system operation. This includes log files, spool directories for printers and mail, temporary files that need to persist across reboots, and other dynamic data.

Understanding the purpose of each of these directories is essential for navigating the Linux filesystem effectively. It also helps you understand where to find specific types of files and how the system is organized overall. When you're working with files and directories in Linux, you'll often use absolute or relative paths to refer to their locations. An absolute path specifies the exact location of a file or directory, starting from the root directory. For example, the absolute path /home/john/Documents/report.txt refers to the file "report.txt" located in the "Documents" directory within the "john" user's home directory.

A relative path, on the other hand, specifies the location of a file or directory relative to the current working directory. The current working directory is the directory you are currently "in" when you're using the command line. For example, if your current working directory is /home/john, the relative path

Documents/report.txt refers to the same file as the absolute path above. Two special symbols are used in relative paths: "." (dot) and ".." (double dot). A single dot represents the current working directory, while a double dot represents the parent directory (the directory one level above the current one).

For example, if your current working directory is /home/john/Documents, the relative path ../Downloads refers to the /home/john/Downloads directory. Navigating the filesystem using the command line is a fundamental skill in Linux. The cd command, which stands for "change directory," is used to move between directories. For example,

```
cd /usr/bin
```

will change the current working directory to /usr/bin.

```
cd ..
```

will move up one level to the parent directory, and

```
cd
```

without any arguments will take you to your home directory.

The pwd command, which stands for "print working directory," displays the absolute path of the current working directory. This can be useful when you're not sure where you are in the filesystem hierarchy. The ls command, which we'll cover in more detail in a later chapter, is used to list the contents of a directory. By default, it lists the files and subdirectories in the current working directory. You can also specify a directory path as an argument to list the contents of a specific directory.

For example,

```
ls /etc
```

will list the files and subdirectories in the /etc directory. File permissions are another important aspect of the Linux filesystem.

Each file and directory has a set of permissions that determine who can read, write, or execute it. Permissions are divided into three categories: owner, group, and others. The owner is the user who created the file or directory. The group is a set of users who have been granted access to the file or directory.

Others refer to all other users on the system. For each category, there are three types of permissions: read (r), write (w), and execute (x). Read permission allows a user to view the contents of a file or list the contents of a directory. Write permission allows a user to modify a file or create, delete, or rename files within a directory. Execute permission allows a user to run a file as a program or, in the case of a directory, access its contents.

File permissions are represented by a string of nine characters, divided into three sets of three. The first set represents the owner's permissions, the second set represents the group's permissions, and the third set represents the permissions for others. For example, the permission string "rw-r--r--" means that the owner has read and write permissions, while the group and others have only read permission. We'll delve deeper into file permissions and how to manage them in a later chapter.

The Linux filesystem also supports different types of files, including regular files, directories, symbolic links, and special device files. Regular files are the most common type and contain data such as text, images, or programs. Directories are special files that contain lists of other files and directories. Symbolic links, also known as soft links, are files that point to other files or directories. They are similar to shortcuts in other operating systems.

When you access a symbolic link, the operating system automatically redirects you to the target file or directory. Special device files, as mentioned earlier, represent hardware devices and allow the operating system to interact with them. In addition to the standard filesystem hierarchy, Linux also supports various filesystem types, such as ext4, XFS, and Btrfs. Each filesystem type has its own characteristics, features, and performance tradeoffs. The ext4 filesystem is the most commonly used filesystem type in Linux and is the default for many distributions.

It's a journaling filesystem, which means it keeps a log of changes before they are written to the disk, helping to prevent data loss in case of a system crash or power failure. XFS is another popular journaling filesystem that is known for its performance and scalability, particularly with large filesystems. Btrfs is a more modern filesystem that offers advanced features such as snapshots, subvolumes, and built-in data integrity checking. The choice of filesystem type depends on the specific needs of the system and the workload it will handle.

As you work with Linux, you'll become more familiar with the filesystem and its nuances. You'll learn how to create, delete, and manage files and directories; how to navigate the filesystem using the command line; and how to understand and modify file permissions. You'll also gain a deeper understanding of the different types of files and filesystems and how they are used in Linux. Mastering the Linux filesystem is a crucial step in becoming proficient with the operating system.

It's the foundation upon which everything else is built, and a solid understanding of its structure and organization will make you a more effective and confident Linux user. Whether you're managing files, configuring the system, or troubleshooting issues, a strong grasp of the filesystem will prove invaluable. As you continue your Linux journey, you'll find that the filesystem is not just a static structure but a dynamic and evolving entity. It reflects the state of your system, the software you've installed, and the data you've created.

It's a living, breathing part of the operating system that responds to your commands and adapts to your needs. With practice and exploration, you'll become intimately familiar with the intricacies of the Linux filesystem. You'll learn how to leverage its power to manage your data, organize your work, and customize your system to your exact specifications. And as you delve deeper into the world of Linux, you'll discover that the filesystem is not just a technical detail but a fundamental part of what makes Linux such a powerful and versatile operating system.

CHAPTER THREE: Navigating the Command Line

In this chapter, we'll delve into the world of the command-line interface (CLI), also known as the terminal or shell. While graphical user interfaces (GUIs) are great for everyday tasks, the command line offers a level of control and efficiency that is unmatched. By typing commands into the terminal, you can interact directly with the operating system, perform complex operations, automate tasks, and troubleshoot issues with precision. Mastering the command line is an essential skill for any Linux user, and it will significantly boost your productivity and understanding of the system. When you first open the terminal, you'll be presented with a prompt, which typically displays your username, the hostname of your computer, and the current working directory. The prompt usually ends with a dollar sign ($) for regular users or a hash symbol (#) for the root user.

The current working directory is the directory you are currently "in" within the filesystem hierarchy. When you first log in, the current working directory is usually your home directory. To navigate the filesystem using the command line, you'll use a variety of commands. The most basic command for moving around is `cd`, which stands for "change directory." To change to a specific directory, you can type `cd` followed by the path to the directory. For example, to change to the /usr/bin directory, you would type

```
cd /usr/bin
```

. Remember that absolute paths start from the root directory (/), while relative paths start from the current working directory.

If you want to move up one level in the directory hierarchy, you can use `cd ..`. The double dot (..) represents the parent directory. For example, if your current working directory is /home/john/Documents, typing

```
cd  ..
```

will take you to /home/john. To quickly return to your home directory from anywhere in the filesystem, you can simply type `cd` without any arguments or `cd  ~`, where the tilde (~) is a shortcut for your home directory. The `pwd` command, which stands for "print working directory," displays the absolute path of the current working directory. This can be useful when you're not sure where you are in the filesystem or when you need to specify the full path to a file or directory.

Another essential command for navigating the command line is `ls`, which lists the contents of a directory. By default, `ls` lists the files and subdirectories in the current working directory. You can also specify a directory path as an argument to list the contents of a specific directory. For example,

```
ls /etc
```

will list the files and subdirectories in the /etc directory. The `ls` command has many options that modify its behavior. For example, `ls  -l` displays the contents in a long listing format, which includes additional information such as file permissions, ownership, size, and modification time.

The `ls  -a` option shows all files, including hidden files that start with a dot (.). In Linux, files that start with a dot are considered hidden and are not displayed by default. The `ls  -h` option, when used with `-l`, displays file sizes in a human-readable format (e.g., 1K, 234M, 2G). You can combine multiple options, such as `ls  -lah`, to get a long listing of all files with human-readable sizes. When working with commands, it's important to understand the concept of command-line arguments and options. Arguments are the values you provide to a command, such as a filename or directory path.

Options, also known as flags or switches, modify the behavior of a command. Options usually start with one or two hyphens, such as `-l` or `--help`. Many commands have a `--help` option that displays a brief description of the command and its usage. As you type commands, you can use the Tab key for autocompletion. If you start typing a command or filename and press Tab, the shell will attempt to complete it automatically. If there are multiple possibilities, pressing Tab twice will display a list of options. Autocompletion saves time and reduces typing errors, especially when dealing with long filenames or complex commands.

The command line also keeps a history of the commands you've entered. You can use the up and down arrow keys to navigate through the command history. This allows you to quickly recall and re-execute previous commands without having to retype them. You can also use the `history` command to view a numbered list of your command history. To re-run a specific command from the history, you can type an exclamation mark (!) followed by the command number. For example, `!123` would re-execute the command numbered 123 in the history.

Another useful feature is the ability to search through your command history. By pressing Ctrl+R, you can enter reverse-i-search mode. As you start typing, the shell will display the most recent command that matches your input. You can press Ctrl+R again to cycle through matching commands. Once you've found the command you want, you can press Enter to execute it or Esc to cancel the search. Sometimes, you might need to run a command with administrative privileges, especially when performing system-level tasks such as installing software or modifying system configuration files.

In such cases, you can use the `sudo` command, which stands for "superuser do." By prefixing a command with `sudo`, you can execute it with root privileges. For example,

```
sudo apt update
```

will run the `apt update` command as the root user. When you use `sudo`, you'll be prompted to enter your password to confirm your identity. It's important to use `sudo` judiciously and only when necessary, as running commands with root privileges can have significant consequences if misused. File manipulation is a common task on the command line.

The cp command is used to copy files and directories. The basic syntax is

```
cp source destination
```

, where "source" is the file or directory you want to copy, and "destination" is the location where you want to copy it. For example,

```
cp report.txt backup/
```

will copy the file "report.txt" to the "backup" directory. To copy a directory, you need to use the -r (recursive) option. For example,

```
cp -r Documents MyDocs
```

will copy the "Documents" directory and all its contents to a new directory called "MyDocs".

The mv command is used to move or rename files and directories. The syntax is similar to cp:

```
mv source destination
```

. If you specify a directory as the destination, the source file or directory will be moved into that directory. If you specify a new filename as the destination, the source file or directory will be renamed. For example,

```
mv report.txt archive/
```

will move "report.txt" to the "archive" directory, while

```
mv oldname.txt newname.txt
```

will rename "oldname.txt" to "newname.txt".

The `rm` command is used to remove (delete) files and directories. Be very careful when using `rm`, as deleted files are not easily recoverable. The basic syntax is

```
rm file
```

, where "file" is the name of the file you want to delete. For example,

```
rm unwanted.txt
```

will delete the file "unwanted.txt". To remove a directory, you need to use the `-r` (recursive) option. For example,

```
rm -r old_project/
```

will delete the directory "old_project" and all its contents.

The `-f` (force) option can be used to suppress confirmation prompts when deleting files. However, use this option with extreme caution, as it can lead to accidental data loss. It's a good practice to double-check the `rm` command before executing it, especially when using wildcards or the `-rf` option. To create a new directory, you can use the `mkdir` command, which stands for "make directory." The syntax is

```
mkdir directory_name
```

. For example,

```
mkdir NewProject
```

will create a new directory called "NewProject" in the current working directory.

You can also create multiple directories at once or create nested directories using the `-p` option. For example,

```
mkdir -p Projects/2023/ProjectA
```

will create the directory structure "Projects/2023/ProjectA", creating any missing parent directories as needed. To create an empty file, you can use the `touch` command. The syntax is

```
touch filename
```

. For example,

```
touch newfile.txt
```

will create an empty file named "newfile.txt" in the current working directory. If the file already exists, `touch` will update its modification time without changing its contents.

The `cat` command, short for "concatenate," is used to display the contents of a file on the terminal. The syntax is

```
cat filename
```

. For example,

```
cat mydocument.txt
```

will display the contents of "mydocument.txt". `cat` can also be used to concatenate multiple files and display their combined output. For example,

```
cat file1.txt file2.txt
```

will display the contents of "file1.txt" followed by "file2.txt". However, for large files, it's often more practical to use commands like `less` or `more`, which allow you to view the file one page at a time.

The `less` command is a pager that allows you to view text files in a scrollable manner. The syntax is

```
less filename
```

. For example,

```
less mylongdocument.txt
```

will open "mylongdocument.txt" in the `less` pager. You can use the arrow keys, Page Up, and Page Down to navigate the file. Press q to quit `less` and return to the command prompt. `less` has many features, such as searching for text within the file using / followed by the search term. The `head` and `tail` commands are used to display the beginning or end of a file, respectively.

By default, they show the first or last 10 lines. The syntax is

```
head filename
```

or

```
tail filename
```

. For example,

```
head mylog.txt
```

will display the first 10 lines of "mylog.txt", while

```
tail mylog.txt
```

will display the last 10 lines. You can use the -n option to specify the number of lines to display. For example,

```
head -n 5 mylog.txt
```

will show the first 5 lines. The `tail` command has a useful -f (follow) option that displays the last lines of a file and updates the output as the file grows.

This is particularly useful for monitoring log files in real-time. For example,

```
tail -f /var/log/syslog
```

will display the last lines of the system log and continuously update the output as new log entries are written. To stop following the file, press Ctrl+C. Wildcards are special characters that allow you to match multiple files based on patterns. The most common wildcard is the asterisk (), *which matches any sequence of characters. For example,*

```
ls .txt
```

will list all files in the current directory that end with ".txt".

The question mark (?) wildcard matches any single character. For example,

```
ls report?.txt
```

will match files like "report1.txt", "reportA.txt", but not "report10.txt". You can use wildcards with many commands, such as cp, mv, and rm. However, be cautious when using wildcards with destructive commands like rm, as you could accidentally delete more files than intended. Input and output redirection is a powerful feature of the command line that allows you to control where a command gets its input from and where it sends its output.

By default, most commands read input from the keyboard (standard input) and send output to the terminal (standard output). However, you can redirect input and output using special operators. The greater-than symbol (>) redirects the output of a command to a file, overwriting its contents. For example,

```
ls > filelist.txt
```

will write the output of ls to "filelist.txt". The double greater-than symbol (>>) appends the output of a command to a file without overwriting it.

For example,

```
date >> log.txt
```

will append the current date and time to "log.txt". The less-than symbol (<) redirects the input of a command from a file. For example,

```
sort < words.txt
```

will read the contents of "words.txt" and pass them as input to the sort command. Pipes (|) are used to connect the output of one command to the input of another command. This allows you to chain multiple commands together to perform complex operations. For example,

```
ls -l | grep ".txt"
```

will list all files in the long format and then pass the output to grep, which will filter the lines containing ".txt".

This effectively lists only text files. Command-line editing allows you to modify commands before executing them. You can use the left and right arrow keys to move the cursor within the command line. The Home and End keys move the cursor to the beginning or end of the line, respectively. The Backspace key deletes the character before the cursor, while the Delete key deletes the character under the cursor. You can also use Ctrl+U to delete from the cursor to the beginning of the line and Ctrl+K to delete from the cursor to the end of the line.

These editing features can significantly speed up your command-line workflow, especially when correcting mistakes or modifying complex commands. The clear command clears the terminal screen, removing all previous output and leaving only the prompt at the top. This can be useful when the screen becomes cluttered or when you want to start with a clean slate. You can also use the keyboard shortcut Ctrl+L to achieve the same result. As you become more proficient with the command line, you'll discover many more commands and techniques for navigating and manipulating the Linux filesystem.

The command line is a vast and powerful tool, and mastering it takes time and practice. Don't be afraid to experiment, try new commands, and explore their options. Refer to the manual pages (using the `man` command) for detailed information about each command and its usage. The more you use the command line, the more comfortable and efficient you'll become. You'll learn how to combine commands, use wildcards effectively, and leverage input/output redirection and pipes to perform complex tasks with just a few keystrokes.

The command line is not just a tool for system administrators or power users; it's an essential part of the Linux experience. It allows you to interact with the operating system in a direct and powerful way, unlocking a level of control and flexibility that is simply not possible with graphical interfaces alone. As you continue your Linux journey, embrace the command line and make it your own. Customize your prompt, create aliases for frequently used commands, and explore the vast ecosystem of command-line utilities. The more you invest in learning the command line, the more rewarding your Linux experience will be.

CHAPTER FOUR: Essential Command Line Tools

This chapter introduces some of the most commonly used and essential command-line tools in Linux. These tools will help you perform a wide range of tasks, from managing files and directories to searching for text, manipulating data, and monitoring system resources. As you become more familiar with these tools, you'll find that they are indispensable for working efficiently in the Linux environment. These tools are designed to be powerful, flexible, and composable, allowing you to combine them in various ways to accomplish complex tasks.

One of the most fundamental tools for working with text files is grep, which stands for "global regular expression print." grep allows you to search for specific patterns within files or input streams. The basic syntax is

```
grep pattern file
```

, where "pattern" is the text or regular expression you want to search for, and "file" is the name of the file you want to search within. For example,

```
grep "error" /var/log/syslog
```

will search for the word "error" in the syslog file and display any lines that contain it.

grep has many options that enhance its functionality. The -i option performs a case-insensitive search, while the -n option displays the line numbers along with the matching lines. The -r option allows you to search recursively through directories. For example,

```
grep -r "myfunction" /home/john/projects
```

will search for "myfunction" in all files within the /home/john/projects directory and its subdirectories. The -v option inverts the match, displaying lines that do not contain the pattern. You can also use regular expressions with grep to perform more complex searches.

Regular expressions are sequences of characters that define a search pattern. For example,

```
grep "^[0-9]" myfile.txt
```

will search for lines that start with a digit. Mastering regular expressions takes time and practice, but they are an incredibly powerful tool for text processing. grep is often used in combination with pipes to filter the output of other commands. For example,

```
ps aux | grep "firefox"
```

will list all running processes and then filter the output to show only lines containing "firefox". This effectively displays only the processes related to the Firefox web browser.

Another essential tool for working with text is sed, which stands for "stream editor." sed allows you to perform text transformations on an input stream or file. It reads the input line by line, applies the specified commands, and outputs the modified lines. The most common use of sed is for substitution. The syntax for substitution is

```
sed 's/pattern/replacement/g' file
```

, where "pattern" is the text or regular expression you want to replace, "replacement" is the text you want to replace it with, and "file" is the name of the file you want to operate on.

The s command stands for "substitute," and the g flag means "global," indicating that all occurrences on each line should be replaced. For example,

```
sed 's/red/blue/g' colors.txt
```

will replace all occurrences of "red" with "blue" in the "colors.txt" file. By default, `sed` prints the modified output to the terminal. To modify the file in place, you can use the `-i` option. However, it's a good practice to create a backup of the file before using `sed -i`, as the changes are irreversible.

`sed` can perform many other text transformations, such as deleting lines, inserting text, and changing specific lines. Like `grep`, `sed` supports regular expressions, making it a powerful tool for manipulating text. The `awk` command is another powerful text processing tool. It is a scripting language designed for text processing and data extraction. `awk` reads an input file line by line, splits each line into fields, and performs actions based on specified patterns. The basic syntax of an `awk` command is

```
awk 'pattern { action }' file
```

, where "pattern" is a condition to match, "action" is the set of commands to execute when the pattern is matched, and "file" is the name of the input file.

If the pattern is omitted, the action is performed for every line. The fields in each line are represented by variables $1, $2, $3, and so on, where $1 is the first field, $2 is the second field, and so forth. The variable $0 represents the entire line. For example,

```
awk '{ print $1, $3 }' data.txt
```

will print the first and third fields of each line in "data.txt". `awk` can perform various operations on fields, such as arithmetic calculations, string manipulation, and conditional statements. You can also use built-in variables like NR (current line number) and NF (number of fields in the current line) to perform more complex actions.

`awk` is often used for data extraction and reporting. For example, you can use it to parse log files, extract specific fields, and generate formatted reports. It's a versatile tool that can handle complex text processing tasks with concise and expressive scripts. The `sort` command is used to sort lines of text files. By default, it sorts lines in ascending order based on their ASCII values. The basic syntax is

```
sort file
```

, where "file" is the name of the file you want to sort. For example,

```
sort names.txt
```

will sort the lines in "names.txt" alphabetically.

`sort` has several options to modify its behavior. The `-r` option reverses the sort order, while the `-n` option sorts lines numerically instead of alphabetically. The `-k` option allows you to specify a key field for sorting. For example,

```
sort -k2 data.txt
```

will sort the lines in "data.txt" based on the second field. You can also use `sort` with pipes to sort the output of other commands. For example,

```
ls -l | sort -nk5
```

will list files in the long format and sort them numerically based on the fifth field, which represents the file size. This effectively sorts files by size in ascending order.

The `uniq` command is used to filter out repeated lines in a file or input stream. It only removes consecutive duplicate lines, so it's often used in conjunction with `sort`. The basic syntax is

```
uniq file
```

, where "file" is the name of the file you want to process. For example, if "data.txt" contains the lines "apple", "banana", "apple", "apple", "orange", "banana", running

```
uniq data.txt
```

will output "apple", "banana", "apple", "orange", "banana". Notice that only the consecutive duplicate "apple" lines were reduced to a single "apple".

To remove all duplicate lines, you can first sort the file using sort and then pipe the output to uniq. For example,

```
sort data.txt | uniq
```

will output "apple", "banana", "orange". uniq has several options, such as -c to count the number of occurrences of each line and -d to display only duplicate lines. The wc command, which stands for "word count," is used to count the number of lines, words, and characters in a file. The basic syntax is

```
wc file
```

, where "file" is the name of the file you want to analyze.

For example,

```
wc mydocument.txt
```

might output "10 45 284 mydocument.txt", indicating that the file has 10 lines, 45 words, and 284 characters. wc has options to display only specific counts. The -l option displays the number of lines, the -w option displays the number of words, and the -c option displays the number of characters (bytes). You can combine wc with other commands using pipes to count the output of those commands. For example,

```
ls -l | wc -l
```

will count the number of lines in the output of ls -l, effectively counting the number of files in the current directory.

The find command is a powerful tool for searching for files and directories based on various criteria. The basic syntax is

```
find directory options expression
```

, where "directory" is the starting directory for the search, "options" modify the behavior of `find`, and "expression" specifies the search criteria. For example,

```
find /home -name "*.txt"
```

will search for all files ending with ".txt" in the /home directory and its subdirectories. The `-name` option specifies a pattern to match against filenames.

`find` has many other options for searching based on file type, size, modification time, permissions, and more. For example,

```
find /var/log -type f -mtime -7
```

will search for all regular files in /var/log that were modified in the last 7 days. You can also use `find` to perform actions on the files it finds. The `-exec` option allows you to execute a command on each found file. For example,

```
find . -name "*.bak" -exec rm {} \;
```

will search for all files ending with ".bak" in the current directory and its subdirectories and delete them using the `rm` command.

The { } is a placeholder that is replaced with the name of each found file, and the \; terminates the `-exec` command. The `find` command is a versatile tool that can be used for various file management tasks, such as locating specific files, cleaning up temporary files, and performing batch operations on files that match certain criteria. It's an essential tool for system administrators and power users. The `locate` command provides a faster way to find files by searching a pre-built database of filenames.

The database is typically updated periodically by a background process. The basic syntax is

```
locate pattern
```

, where "pattern" is the filename or pattern you want to search for. For example,

```
locate mydocument.txt
```

will quickly find all files named "mydocument.txt" in the database. `locate` is faster than `find` because it searches the database instead of traversing the filesystem. However, the results might not be up-to-date if the database hasn't been updated recently.

The `updatedb` command can be used to manually update the locate database. It's typically run with `sudo` privileges, as it requires access to the entire filesystem. The `which` command is used to locate the executable file associated with a given command. It searches the directories specified in the `PATH` environment variable and displays the full path to the first executable file that matches the command name. The basic syntax is

```
which command
```

, where "command" is the name of the command you want to locate.

For example,

```
which python
```

might output "/usr/bin/python", indicating that the `python` executable is located in /usr/bin. `which` is useful for determining which version of a command will be executed when you type its name in the terminal. It can also help troubleshoot issues related to command not found errors by verifying that the command is installed and located in a directory listed in the `PATH`. The `whereis` command is similar to `which`, but it also searches for source files and manual pages related to the command.

The `whatis` command displays a one-line description of a command, extracted from its manual page. The `man` command, which we introduced in the previous chapter, is used to display the manual pages for commands and other system components. Manual pages, also known as man pages, provide detailed documentation about commands, including their options, usage, and examples. The basic syntax is

```
man command
```

, where "command" is the name of the command you want to learn about.

For example,

```
man ls
```

will display the manual page for the `ls` command. Man pages are organized into sections, such as user commands, system calls, library functions, and file formats. You can specify the section number before the command name to view a specific section. For example,

```
man 2 read
```

will display the manual page for the `read` system call in section 2. Within the man page, you can use the arrow keys, Page Up, and Page Down to navigate the content.

Press / to search for a specific term within the page, and press q to quit the man page and return to the command prompt. The `info` command is another documentation system that provides more detailed information than man pages for some commands and programs, particularly those from the GNU project. Info pages are organized as nodes that can be navigated using hyperlinks. The basic syntax is

```
info command
```

, where "command" is the name of the command you want to learn about.

For example,

```
info coreutils
```

will display the info page for the GNU core utilities, which includes many essential command-line tools. Within the info page, you can use the arrow keys, Tab, and Enter to navigate the nodes. Press q to quit the info page and return to the command prompt. The apropos command is used to search the manual page descriptions for a given keyword. It's helpful when you're not sure which command you need but have a general idea of what you want to do.

The basic syntax is

```
apropos keyword
```

, where "keyword" is the term you want to search for. For example,

```
apropos "copy files"
```

will list commands related to copying files, along with their one-line descriptions. apropos is equivalent to using man -k. The alias command allows you to create custom shortcuts for commands. An alias is an alternative name for a command, often used to create shorter or more memorable names for frequently used commands or to provide default options for a command.

The basic syntax for creating an alias is

```
alias name='command'
```

, where "name" is the alias you want to create, and "command" is the command it should execute. For example,

```
alias ll='ls -l'
```

will create an alias named ll that executes ls -l. Now, whenever you type ll in the terminal, it will run ls -l. Aliases are typically defined in shell configuration files, such as ~/.bashrc or ~/.bash_aliases, so they persist across sessions.

To list all defined aliases, you can run alias without any arguments. To remove an alias, you can use the unalias command followed by the alias name. For example,

```
unalias ll
```

will remove the ll alias. The echo command is used to display a line of text or the value of a variable. It's often used in shell scripts for printing messages or debugging. The basic syntax is

```
echo text
```

, where "text" is the string you want to display.

For example,

```
echo "Hello, world!"
```

will print "Hello, world!" to the terminal. You can also use echo to display the value of environment variables. For example,

```
echo $PATH
```

will print the value of the PATH variable. The export command is used to set environment variables in the current shell session. Environment variables are dynamic values that can affect the behavior of running processes. The basic syntax is

```
export VARNAME=value
```

, where "VARNAME" is the name of the variable, and "value" is the value you want to assign to it.

For example,

```
export MYVAR="Hello"
```

will set the environment variable MYVAR to "Hello". To make an environment variable available to child processes, you need to export it. Exported variables are inherited by child processes, while non-exported variables are only available in the current shell. To list all environment variables, you can use the printenv or env command. These commands, along with those discussed previously in this chapter and earlier chapters are just a small selection of the many powerful tools available in the Linux command-line environment. Each tool has its own set of options, features, and nuances.

As you continue to explore and use these tools, you'll discover their versatility and how they can be combined to perform complex tasks. You'll learn how to use pipes and redirection to connect commands, how to use regular expressions to search and manipulate text, and how to use shell scripting to automate tasks. Mastering the command line takes time and practice, but it's a worthwhile investment. The command line is a fundamental part of the Linux experience, and it provides a level of control and efficiency that is unmatched by graphical interfaces alone.

As you become more proficient with these essential command-line tools, you'll find that they are not just tools for system administrators or power users but for anyone who wants to harness the full potential of the Linux operating system. Whether you're managing files, processing data, monitoring system resources, or automating tasks, these tools will become an indispensable part of your Linux toolkit. Embrace the power of the command line, and you'll unlock a whole new level of productivity and control over your Linux system. And remember, the best way to learn these tools is by using them. Experiment, try different options, and don't be afraid to make mistakes.

CHAPTER FIVE: Working with Files and Directories

This chapter delves into the practical aspects of managing files and directories in Linux. We'll explore essential commands for creating, deleting, copying, moving, and renaming files and directories. You'll learn how to use wildcards to perform operations on multiple files at once and how to leverage input/output redirection and pipes to manipulate file contents. Understanding these operations is crucial for effectively managing your data and working efficiently in the Linux environment. File management is a fundamental aspect of using any operating system, and Linux provides a rich set of command-line tools for this purpose.

The `touch` command, as we briefly saw in the previous chapter, is used to create empty files. The basic syntax is

```
touch filename
```

, where "filename" is the name of the file you want to create. For example,

```
touch newfile.txt
```

will create an empty file named "newfile.txt" in the current working directory. If the file already exists, `touch` will update its modification time without changing its contents. This can be useful for creating placeholder files or updating timestamps.

The `mkdir` command, which stands for "make directory," is used to create new directories. The basic syntax is

```
mkdir directory_name
```

. For example,

```
mkdir NewFolder
```

will create a new directory called "NewFolder" in the current working directory. You can also create multiple directories at once by specifying their names as separate arguments. For example,

```
mkdir Folder1 Folder2 Folder3
```

will create three new directories named "Folder1", "Folder2", and "Folder3".

To create nested directories in a single command, you can use the -p option. This option tells mkdir to create any missing parent directories as needed. For example,

```
mkdir -p Projects/2023/ProjectA
```

will create the directory structure "Projects/2023/ProjectA", creating the "Projects" and "2023" directories if they don't already exist. This is particularly useful when you need to create a deep directory hierarchy without having to issue multiple mkdir commands.

The cp command is used to copy files and directories. The basic syntax for copying a file is

```
cp source_file destination
```

, where "source_file" is the name of the file you want to copy, and "destination" is the location where you want to copy it. For example,

```
cp document.txt backup/
```

will copy "document.txt" to the "backup" directory. If you specify a filename as the destination, the copied file will have that name. For example,

```
cp report.txt report_copy.txt
```

will create a copy of "report.txt" named "report_copy.txt" in the same directory.

To copy a directory, you need to use the `-r` (recursive) option. This option tells `cp` to copy the directory and all its contents, including subdirectories. For example,

```
cp -r Documents MyDocs
```

will copy the "Documents" directory and all its contents to a new directory called "MyDocs". It's important to note that if the destination directory already exists, the source directory will be copied inside it. If you want to merge the contents of the source directory into the destination directory, you can use a trailing slash with the source directory name.

The `mv` command is used to move or rename files and directories. The basic syntax for moving a file is

```
mv source destination
```

, where "source" is the file or directory you want to move, and "destination" is the location where you want to move it. For example,

```
mv notes.txt archive/
```

will move "notes.txt" to the "archive" directory. If you specify a directory as the destination, the source file or directory will be moved into that directory.

To rename a file or directory, you can use `mv` with the new name as the destination. For example,

```
mv oldname.txt newname.txt
```

will rename "oldname.txt" to "newname.txt". When moving files between different filesystems or partitions, `mv` essentially performs a copy and delete operation. The file is first copied to the destination, and then the original file is deleted. This can take longer than moving files within the same filesystem, as the data needs to be physically copied.

The `rm` command is used to remove (delete) files and directories. Be very cautious when using `rm`, as deleted files are not easily recoverable. Unlike some graphical file managers that have a trash bin or recycle bin, files deleted with `rm` are permanently removed. The basic syntax for deleting a file is

```
rm file
```

, where "file" is the name of the file you want to delete. For example,

```
rm unwanted.txt
```

will delete the file "unwanted.txt".

To remove a directory, you need to use the `-r` (recursive) option. For example,

```
rm -r old_project/
```

will delete the directory "old_project" and all its contents, including subdirectories. The `-f` (force) option can be used to suppress confirmation prompts when deleting files. However, use this option with extreme caution, as it can lead to accidental data loss. It's a good practice to double-check the `rm` command before executing it, especially when using wildcards or the `-rf` option.

Wildcards are special characters that allow you to match multiple files based on patterns. The most common wildcard is the asterisk (), *which matches any sequence of characters. For example,*

```
rm .txt
```

will delete all files in the current directory that end with ".txt". The question mark (?) wildcard matches any single character. For example,

```
cp report?.txt backup/
```

will copy files like "report1.txt" and "reportA.txt" to the "backup" directory, but not "report10.txt".

You can use wildcards with many commands, such as cp, mv, and rm. However, be particularly careful when using wildcards with destructive commands like rm. It's easy to accidentally delete more files than intended if you're not careful with your patterns. Always double-check your wildcard expressions before executing rm, and consider using the -i (interactive) option to be prompted for confirmation before each deletion.

Input/output redirection is a powerful feature that allows you to control where a command gets its input from and where it sends its output. By default, most commands read input from the keyboard (standard input) and send output to the terminal (standard output). However, you can redirect input and output using special operators. The greater-than symbol (>) redirects the output of a command to a file, overwriting its contents.

For example,

```
ls > filelist.txt
```

will write the output of the ls command to a file named "filelist.txt". If "filelist.txt" already exists, its contents will be overwritten. The double greater-than symbol (>>) appends the output of a command to a file without overwriting it. For example,

```
date >> log.txt
```

will append the current date and time to the end of "log.txt". If "log.txt" doesn't exist, it will be created.

The less-than symbol (<) redirects the input of a command from a file. For example,

```
sort < words.txt
```

will read the contents of "words.txt" and pass them as input to the sort command, which will then sort the lines alphabetically.

Pipes (|) are used to connect the output of one command to the input of another command. This allows you to chain multiple commands together to perform complex operations.

For example,

```
ls -l | grep ".txt"
```

will list all files in the long format and then pass the output to `grep`, which will filter the lines containing ".txt". This effectively lists only text files. You can chain multiple commands using pipes to create powerful data processing pipelines. For example,

```
cat access.log | awk '{print $1}' | sort |
uniq -c | sort -nr
```

will process an access log file, extract the first field (typically the IP address), sort the IP addresses, count the unique occurrences of each IP, and then sort the results in reverse numerical order to show the most frequent visitors.

The `ln` command is used to create links between files. There are two types of links in Linux: hard links and symbolic links (also known as soft links). A hard link is essentially an additional name for an existing file. Hard links share the same inode (data structure that stores file metadata) and data blocks as the original file. They are indistinguishable from the original file and act as if they were separate copies, even though they point to the same data on disk.

To create a hard link, you can use the `ln` command followed by the existing file and the desired link name. For example,

```
ln original.txt hardlink.txt
```

will create a hard link named "hardlink.txt" that points to the same data as "original.txt". If you modify either "original.txt" or "hardlink.txt", the changes will be reflected in both files because they share the same data. However, if you delete one of the hard links, the other link will still work, and the data will only be deleted when all links to it are removed.

A symbolic link, on the other hand, is a separate file that acts as a pointer to another file or directory. It's similar to a shortcut in other operating systems. Symbolic links have their own inode and data blocks, but the data block simply contains the path to the target file or directory. To create a symbolic link, you use the `ln` command with the `-s` option, followed by the target file or directory and the desired link name.

For example,

```
ln -s /path/to/target linkname
```

will create a symbolic link named "linkname" that points to "/path/to/target". If you access "linkname", the operating system will automatically redirect you to the target. Unlike hard links, symbolic links can point to files or directories on different filesystems or partitions. They can also point to directories, whereas hard links can only point to regular files. If you delete a symbolic link, it doesn't affect the target file or directory.

However, if you delete the target of a symbolic link, the link becomes "broken" or "dangling" because it points to a non-existent location. Symbolic links are often used to create convenient shortcuts to frequently accessed files or directories, to create alternative names for files, or to provide compatibility with programs that expect files to be in specific locations. They are a flexible tool for organizing and managing files in Linux.

The `chmod` command is used to change the permissions of files and directories. As we discussed in Chapter 2, each file and directory has a set of permissions that determine who can read, write, or execute it. Permissions are divided into three categories: owner, group, and others. For each category, there are three types of permissions: read (r), write (w), and execute (x). `chmod` allows you to modify these permissions using either symbolic notation or octal notation.

Symbolic notation uses letters to represent permissions and categories. The letters `u`, `g`, `o`, and `a` represent the owner (user), group, others, and all (u+g+o), respectively. The symbols +, −, and = are used to add, remove, or set permissions, respectively. For example,

```
chmod u+x script.sh
```

will add execute permission for the owner of "script.sh".

```
chmod go-w myfile.txt
```

will remove write permission for the group and others for "myfile.txt".

```
chmod a=rw data.txt
```

will set read and write permissions for all categories, removing execute permission.

Octal notation uses numbers to represent permissions. Each permission is assigned a numerical value: read (4), write (2), and execute (1). The values are added together to represent the desired permissions for each category. For example, the value 7 (4+2+1) represents read, write, and execute permissions. The first digit represents the owner's permissions, the second digit represents the group's permissions, and the third digit represents the permissions for others.

For example,

```
chmod 755 script.sh
```

will set read, write, and execute permissions for the owner (7), and read and execute permissions for the group and others (5).

```
chmod 644 myfile.txt
```

will set read and write permissions for the owner (6) and read-only permission for the group and others (4). Octal notation is often preferred for its conciseness, especially when setting specific permissions for all categories.

The `chown` command is used to change the ownership of files and directories. Each file and directory has an owner and a group associated with it. The owner is typically the user who created the file, and the group is a set of users who have been granted access to the file. The basic syntax for changing the owner is

```
chown newowner file
```

, where "newowner" is the username of the new owner, and "file" is the name of the file or directory.

For example,

```
chown john document.txt
```

will change the owner of "document.txt" to the user "john". To change the group ownership, you can use the syntax

```
chown :newgroup file
```

or

```
chgrp newgroup file
```

, where "newgroup" is the name of the new group. For example,

```
chown :developers project.c
```

will change the group ownership of "project.c" to the group "developers".

You can also change both the owner and group in a single command using the syntax

```
chown newowner:newgroup file
```

. For example,

```
chown jane:admins config.txt
```

will change the owner of "config.txt" to "jane" and the group to "admins". To recursively change the ownership of a directory and all its contents, you can use the −R option. For example,

```
chown -R sarah:staff myproject/
```

will change the owner of the "myproject" directory and all its files and subdirectories to "sarah" and the group to "staff".

The du command, which stands for "disk usage," is used to display the disk space used by files and directories. The basic syntax is

```
du path
```

, where "path" is the file or directory you want to analyze. If no path is specified, du analyzes the current working directory. By default, du displays the disk usage of each subdirectory recursively, followed by a total for the specified directory.

The output shows the number of disk blocks used by each directory and file. The −h option displays the sizes in a human-readable format, using units like K (kilobytes), M (megabytes), and G (gigabytes). For example,

```
du -h Documents
```

will display the disk usage of the "Documents" directory and its subdirectories in a human-readable format. The −s (summarize) option displays only the total disk usage for the specified directory, without listing each subdirectory.

For example,

```
du -sh /home/john
```

will display the total disk usage of "/home/john" in a human-readable format. The −c (total) option displays a grand total at the end of the output. You can combine du with other commands, such as sort, to analyze disk usage in more detail. For example,

```
du -h /home | sort -rh | head -n 10
```

will display the disk usage of "/home" and its subdirectories, sort the output in reverse human-readable order, and then display the top 10 largest directories.

The df command, which stands for "disk free," is used to display information about file system disk space usage. It shows the amount of disk space used and available on each mounted file system. The basic syntax is

```
df
```

. By default, df displays information for all mounted file systems, including the file system name, total size, used space, available space, usage percentage, and mount point.

The -h option displays the sizes in a human-readable format. For example,

```
df -h
```

will display the disk space usage of all file systems in a human-readable format. The -T option displays the file system type for each entry. The -i option displays inode usage instead of block usage. Inodes are data structures that store information about files, and a file system has a limited number of inodes.

Running out of inodes can prevent you from creating new files, even if there is free space on the disk. You can also specify a file or directory as an argument to df to display information about the file system that contains it. For example,

```
df -h /home
```

will display information about the file system where "/home" is located. df is a useful tool for monitoring disk space usage and identifying file systems that are running low on space.

These commands provide a comprehensive toolkit for managing files and directories in Linux. By mastering these tools, you'll be able to efficiently organize your data, manipulate files, and maintain your system. The ability to use wildcards, redirection, and pipes allows you to perform complex operations with just a few commands, saving time and effort. As you continue to work with Linux, you'll find that these file and directory management skills are essential for a wide range of tasks.

Whether you're a system administrator managing a server, a developer working on a project, or a user organizing your personal files, these commands will be an indispensable part of your daily workflow. The flexibility and power of the Linux command line when it comes to managing files and directories are truly remarkable. With practice, you'll be able to navigate the file system with ease, manipulate files and directories effortlessly, and harness the full potential of the Linux operating system. This knowledge forms a solid foundation for more advanced topics, such as scripting, automation, and system administration, which we'll explore in later chapters.

CHAPTER SIX: User and Group Management

This chapter delves into the essential concepts of user and group management in Linux. It is a crucial aspect of system administration and security. You'll learn how to create, modify, and delete user accounts, how to manage groups, and how to use commands like `sudo` to delegate administrative privileges. Understanding these concepts is fundamental to maintaining a secure and well-organized multi-user environment. In Linux, every user has a unique username and a corresponding user ID (UID). The UID is a numerical identifier that the system uses internally to track user permissions and ownership of files and processes. Each user also belongs to at least one group, which has a group name and a group ID (GID).

Groups are used to manage permissions for multiple users collectively. When a user creates a file, the file is owned by that user and assigned to the user's primary group. Permissions can then be granted to the owner, the group, or all other users. The root user, as mentioned earlier, is the superuser account that has unrestricted access to the entire system. The root user has a UID of 0 and can perform any operation, including modifying system files, installing software, and managing user accounts. It's crucial to use the root account judiciously, as any mistakes made while logged in as root can have far-reaching consequences.

To create a new user account, you can use the `adduser` command followed by the desired username. For example,

```
sudo adduser sarah
```

will create a new user account named "sarah". The `adduser` command is a higher-level utility that performs several actions in one go. It creates the user's home directory, sets up a default shell, and prompts you to enter a password and other optional information for the new user. The useradd command is a lower-level alternative to adduser. It provides more fine-grained control over the user creation process but requires you to specify more options manually. For most cases, adduser is the recommended choice.

When you create a new user with adduser, the system automatically creates a home directory for that user under /home. The home directory is named after the username and serves as the user's personal space for storing files and configuring their environment. For example, the user "sarah" would have a home directory at /home/sarah. The adduser command also creates a primary group for the new user with the same name as the username. For example, when you create the user "sarah", a group named "sarah" is also created. This group initially contains only the user "sarah".

The passwd command is used to set or change a user's password. To set the initial password for a new user, you can use sudo passwd username. For example,

```
sudo passwd sarah
```

will prompt you to enter a new password for the user "sarah". To change your own password, you can simply run passwd without any arguments. It's important to choose strong passwords that are difficult to guess but easy to remember. A strong password typically contains a mix of uppercase and lowercase letters, numbers, and symbols. Avoid using easily guessable information like your name, birthdate, or common words.

The usermod command is used to modify existing user accounts. It allows you to change various user attributes, such as the username, home directory, login shell, and group memberships. For example, to change a user's login shell to /bin/bash, you can use

```
sudo usermod -s /bin/bash john
```

. The -s option specifies the new shell. To change a user's home directory, you can use the -d option along with the -m option to move the contents of the old home directory to the new location. For example,

```
sudo usermod -d /newhome/john -m john
```

will change "john's" home directory to /newhome/john and move the existing files to the new location.

To add a user to an additional group, you can use the -aG options. The -a option stands for "append," and the -G option specifies the group name. For example,

```
sudo usermod -aG developers sarah
```

will add the user "sarah" to the "developers" group without removing her from her existing groups. To change a user's primary group, you can use the -g option followed by the new group name or GID. For example,

```
sudo usermod -g staff john
```

will change "john's" primary group to "staff".

The userdel command is used to delete user accounts. To remove a user, you can simply run sudo userdel username. For example,

```
sudo userdel john
```

will delete the user account "john". By default, userdel does not remove the user's home directory or any files owned by the user outside of their home directory. To remove the user's home directory and mail spool along with the user account, you can use the -r option. For example,

```
sudo userdel -r sarah
```

will delete the user "sarah" and remove her home directory and mail spool.

The `groupadd` command is used to create new groups. The basic syntax is

```
sudo groupadd groupname
```

. For example,

```
sudo groupadd marketing
```

will create a new group named "marketing". When you create a new group, the system assigns it a unique GID that is not already in use. You can specify a specific GID using the `-g` option, but it's generally recommended to let the system choose an available GID.

The `groupmod` command is used to modify existing groups. You can change the group name using the `-n` option. For example,

```
sudo groupmod -n sales marketing
```

will rename the group "marketing" to "sales". You can also change the GID of a group using the `-g` option. However, changing the GID of a group that owns files can lead to permission issues, as the files will still be associated with the old GID.

The `groupdel` command is used to delete groups. The syntax is

```
sudo groupdel groupname
```

. For example,

```
sudo groupdel oldgroup
```

will delete the group "oldgroup". You cannot delete a group that is the primary group of an existing user. You must first change the user's primary group using `usermod` before deleting the group. It's important to be cautious when deleting groups, as it can affect file permissions and access control.

The `/etc/passwd` file is a text file that contains information about each user account on the system. Each line in the file represents a user account and consists of seven fields separated by colons. The fields are: username, password, UID, GID, user information, home directory, and login shell. The password field traditionally contained the user's encrypted password, but nowadays, it usually contains an "x", indicating that the password is stored in the `/etc/shadow` file, which is only readable by the root user for security reasons.

The `/etc/group` file is similar to `/etc/passwd` but contains information about groups. Each line represents a group and consists of four fields: group name, password, GID, and member list. The member list is a comma-separated list of usernames that belong to the group. The `/etc/shadow` file stores the encrypted passwords for user accounts. It is only readable by the root user, providing an additional layer of security. Each line in the file contains nine fields related to the user's password, such as the username, encrypted password, last password change date, minimum password age, maximum password age, and warning period.

The `id` command displays information about a user's identity, including their UID, primary GID, and a list of groups they belong to. If you run `id` without any arguments, it displays information about the current user. You can also specify a username as an argument to view information about a specific user. For example,

```
id sarah
```

will display the UID, primary GID, and group memberships of the user "sarah".

The `groups` command displays the group memberships for a user. If you run `groups` without any arguments, it displays the groups that the current user belongs to. You can also specify a username as an argument to view the group memberships of a specific user. For example,

```
groups john
```

will display the groups that the user "john" belongs to.

The whoami command displays the username of the current user. It's a simple command that can be useful in scripts or when you're not sure which user you're currently logged in as. The w command displays information about currently logged-in users, including their username, terminal, login time, and what they are currently doing. It's a useful tool for monitoring user activity on the system.

The who command is similar to w but provides a more concise output, showing only the username, terminal, and login time for each logged-in user. It can also display the system's boot time when used with the -b option. The last command displays a list of the most recent user logins, including the username, terminal, login time, logout time (if applicable), and the total duration of the session. It reads the information from the /var/log/wtmp file, which keeps a record of all logins and logouts.

The lastlog command displays the most recent login time for each user on the system. It reads the information from the /var/log/lastlog file, which keeps a record of the last login time for each user. The su command, which stands for "substitute user," allows you to temporarily switch to another user account. By default, if you run su without any arguments, it attempts to switch to the root user. You will be prompted to enter the password for the target user.

For example,

```
su - john
```

will switch to the user "john" and load "john's" environment, including their home directory and shell. The - option ensures that the target user's login scripts are executed, providing a full login environment. It's important to use su with caution, especially when switching to the root user. Any commands executed after switching users will be performed with the privileges of the target user.

The sudo command, which we've used in previous examples, allows you to run commands with the privileges of another user, typically the root user. Unlike su, which requires the target user's password, sudo authenticates users with their own password. This provides better accountability, as each sudo invocation is logged with the user's username. The sudo command is configured through the /etc/sudoers file, which specifies which users or groups are allowed to run which commands as which users.

Editing the /etc/sudoers file directly is discouraged. Instead, you should use the visudo command, which provides a safe way to edit the sudoers file. visudo locks the file to prevent multiple simultaneous edits and performs syntax checking before saving the changes. A typical entry in the sudoers file consists of four fields: the user or group who is granted the privilege, the hosts on which the privilege applies, the user as whom the commands can be run, and the commands that can be run.

For example, the entry

```
john ALL=(ALL:ALL) ALL
```

allows the user "john" to run any command as any user on any host. The entry

```
%developers ALL=(ALL:ALL)
/usr/bin/apt,/usr/bin/yum
```

allows members of the "developers" group to run only the apt and yum commands as any user on any host. The % symbol indicates a group name. It's important to carefully configure the sudoers file to grant only the necessary privileges to users and groups. Overly permissive sudo rules can pose a security risk, as they can allow users to execute commands that they should not have access to.

The `chage` command is used to manage password aging information for user accounts. Password aging is a security feature that forces users to change their passwords periodically. The `chage` command allows you to set various parameters related to password aging, such as the minimum number of days between password changes, the maximum number of days a password can be used, the number of days before password expiration that the user will be warned, and the number of days after password expiration that the account will be disabled.

For example,

```
sudo chage -M 90 john
```

will set the maximum password age for the user "john" to 90 days.

```
sudo chage -W 7 john
```

will set the warning period to 7 days before password expiration. To view the current password aging information for a user, you can use the `-l` option. For example,

```
sudo chage -l sarah
```

will display the password aging settings for the user "sarah".

The `getent` command is a versatile tool for retrieving entries from various system databases, including the user and group databases. You can use it to query information from files like /etc/passwd, /etc/group, and /etc/hosts, as well as from network information services like NIS and LDAP. To retrieve all entries from the user database, you can use

```
getent passwd
```

. This will display the contents of the /etc/passwd file. To retrieve information about a specific user, you can specify the username as an argument. For example,

```
getent passwd john
```

will display the entry for the user "john".

Similarly, you can use

```
getent group
```

to retrieve all entries from the group database, and

```
getent group developers
```

to retrieve information about the "developers" group. The `getent` command is particularly useful when dealing with network-based authentication systems, where user and group information is not stored in local files but rather on a central server.

These commands and concepts provide a solid foundation for managing users and groups in Linux. Proper user and group management is essential for maintaining a secure and organized system. By creating separate user accounts for each user, assigning them to appropriate groups, and carefully configuring `sudo` privileges, you can ensure that users have the necessary access to perform their tasks while preventing unauthorized access to sensitive data or system resources. As you continue to work with Linux, you'll find that user and group management is an integral part of system administration. Whether you're setting up a new server, managing a multi-user environment, or simply organizing your personal Linux system, these skills will be invaluable.

CHAPTER SEVEN: File Permissions and Ownership

This chapter delves into the fundamental concepts of file permissions and ownership in Linux. These concepts are crucial for maintaining security, controlling access to files and directories, and ensuring proper collaboration in a multi-user environment. You'll learn how permissions are structured, how to interpret permission strings, and how to modify permissions using both symbolic and octal notation. Additionally, we'll explore the concepts of ownership and how to change the owner and group associated with files and directories. We will also cover special permissions like setuid, setgid, and the sticky bit, which provide advanced access control mechanisms.

In Linux, every file and directory has a set of permissions that determine who can read, write, or execute it. Permissions are divided into three categories: owner, group, and others. The owner is typically the user who created the file or directory. The group is a set of users who have been granted access to the file or directory. Others refer to all other users on the system who are not the owner and do not belong to the group. For each category, there are three types of permissions: read (r), write (w), and execute (x).

Read permission allows a user to view the contents of a file. For directories, read permission allows a user to list the contents of the directory (i.e., see the names of the files and subdirectories within it). Write permission allows a user to modify the contents of a file. For directories, write permission allows a user to create, delete, or rename files within the directory. Note that deleting or renaming a file requires write permission on the directory, not on the file itself. Execute permission allows a user to run a file as a program or script. For directories, execute permission allows a user to enter the directory (i.e., `cd` into it) and access its contents. Without execute permission, a user cannot access files or subdirectories within the directory, even if they have read or write permissions on them.

Permissions are represented by a string of nine characters, divided into three sets of three. The first set represents the owner's permissions, the second set represents the group's permissions, and the third set represents the permissions for others. Each set consists of three characters: r (read), w (write), and x (execute). If a permission is not granted, a hyphen (-) is used in its place. For example, the permission string rw-r--r-- means that the owner has read and write permissions (rw-), while the group and others have only read permission (r--). The string rwxr-xr-x means that the owner has read, write, and execute permissions (rwx), while the group and others have read and execute permissions (r-x).

The ls -l command, which we covered in earlier chapters, displays the permissions of files and directories in the long listing format. The first field of the ls -l output shows the file type and permissions. The first character indicates the file type. A hyphen (-) represents a regular file, d represents a directory, l represents a symbolic link, c represents a character device, and b represents a block device. The next nine characters represent the permissions, as described above. For example, consider the following output of ls -l:

```
-rw-r--r-- 1 john developers 1234 Jan 1
10:00 myfile.txt

drwxr-xr-x 2 sarah staff 4096 Jan 2 15:30
mydir
```

The first line represents a regular file named "myfile.txt" owned by the user "john" and the group "developers". The owner has read and write permissions, while the group and others have only read permission. The second line represents a directory named "mydir" owned by the user "sarah" and the group "staff". The owner has read, write, and execute permissions, while the group and others have read and execute permissions. The chmod command is used to change the permissions of files and directories.

chmod allows you to modify permissions using either symbolic notation or octal notation. Symbolic notation uses letters to represent permissions and categories. The letters u, g, o, and a represent the owner (user), group, others, and all (u+g+o), respectively. The symbols +, −, and = are used to add, remove, or set permissions, respectively. The letters r, w, and x represent read, write, and execute permissions. For example,

```
chmod u+x script.sh
```

will add execute permission for the owner of "script.sh".

```
chmod go-w myfile.txt
```

will remove write permission for the group and others for "myfile.txt".

```
chmod a=rw data.txt
```

will set read and write permissions for all categories (owner, group, and others), removing execute permission if it was previously set. You can combine multiple changes in a single chmod command by separating them with commas. For example,

```
chmod u+x,g+w,o-r script.sh
```

will add execute permission for the owner, add write permission for the group, and remove read permission for others, all for the file "script.sh".

Octal notation uses numbers to represent permissions. Each permission is assigned a numerical value: read (4), write (2), and execute (1). The values are added together to represent the desired permissions for each category. For example, the value 7 (4+2+1) represents read, write, and execute permissions. The first digit represents the owner's permissions, the second digit represents the group's permissions, and the third digit represents the permissions for others. For example,

```
chmod 755 script.sh
```

will set read, write, and execute permissions for the owner (7), and read and execute permissions for the group and others (5).

```
chmod 644 myfile.txt
```

will set read and write permissions for the owner (6) and read-only permission for the group and others (4). Octal notation is often preferred for its conciseness, especially when setting specific permissions for all categories. It's important to choose the appropriate permissions based on the desired level of access and security. Granting excessive permissions can pose a security risk, while overly restrictive permissions can hinder usability. It's generally recommended to follow the principle of least privilege, granting only the minimum permissions necessary for a user or group to perform their tasks.

The chown command is used to change the ownership of files and directories. Each file and directory has an owner and a group associated with it. The owner is typically the user who created the file, and the group is a set of users who have been granted access to the file. The basic syntax for changing the owner is

```
chown newowner file
```

, where "newowner" is the username of the new owner, and "file" is the name of the file or directory. For example,

```
chown john document.txt
```

will change the owner of "document.txt" to the user "john".

To change the group ownership, you can use the syntax

```
chown :newgroup file
```

or

```
chgrp newgroup file
```

, where "newgroup" is the name of the new group. For example,

```
chown :developers project.c
```

will change the group ownership of "project.c" to the group "developers". You can also change both the owner and group in a single command using the syntax

```
chown newowner:newgroup file
```

. For example,

```
chown jane:admins config.txt
```

will change the owner of "config.txt" to "jane" and the group to "admins".

To recursively change the ownership of a directory and all its contents, you can use the -R option. For example,

```
chown -R sarah:staff myproject/
```

will change the owner of the "myproject" directory and all its files and subdirectories to "sarah" and the group to "staff". It's important to note that only the root user can change the owner of a file. Regular users can only change the group ownership of files they own, and only to groups they belong to.

In addition to the standard read, write, and execute permissions, Linux supports special permissions that provide advanced access control mechanisms. These special permissions are setuid (set user ID), setgid (set group ID), and the sticky bit. The setuid permission, when applied to an executable file, allows the file to be executed with the permissions of the file's owner, regardless of who is executing it. This is useful for allowing regular users to perform tasks that require elevated privileges, such as changing their password using the `passwd` command.

The `passwd` command needs to modify the /etc/shadow file, which is typically only writable by the root user. By setting the setuid bit on the `passwd` executable, regular users can run it with the effective UID of root, allowing them to modify their own password entries in /etc/shadow. To set the setuid bit using symbolic notation, you use u+s. For example,

```
chmod u+s myprogram
```

will set the setuid bit on "myprogram". In octal notation, the setuid bit is represented by the value 4 in the thousands place.

For example,

```
chmod 4755 myprogram
```

will set the setuid bit along with read, write, and execute permissions for the owner, and read and execute permissions for the group and others. When the setuid bit is set on an executable file, the s character replaces the x in the owner's execute permission slot when displayed with `ls -l`. For example, -rwsr-xr-x indicates that the setuid bit is set along with the owner's read, write, and execute permissions.

The setgid permission, when applied to an executable file, allows the file to be executed with the permissions of the file's group, regardless of who is executing it. When applied to a directory, setgid causes new files and subdirectories created within it to inherit the group ownership of the directory, rather than the primary group of the user who created them. This is useful for shared directories where multiple users need to collaborate and ensure that files have consistent group ownership.

To set the setgid bit using symbolic notation, you use g+s. For example,

```
chmod g+s shared_dir
```

will set the setgid bit on the directory "shared_dir". In octal notation, the setgid bit is represented by the value 2 in the thousands place. For example,

```
chmod 2775 shared_dir
```

will set the setgid bit along with read, write, and execute permissions for the owner and group, and read and execute permissions for others. When the setgid bit is set on a directory, the s character replaces the x in the group's execute permission slot when displayed with `ls -l`.

For example, `drwxrwsr-x` indicates that the setgid bit is set along with read, write, and execute permissions for the owner and group. The sticky bit, when applied to a directory, restricts file deletion within that directory to the file's owner, the directory's owner, or the root user. This is useful for shared directories like /tmp, where multiple users can create files, but you want to prevent users from deleting each other's files. To set the sticky bit using symbolic notation, you use +t.

For example,

```
chmod +t /tmp
```

will set the sticky bit on the /tmp directory. In octal notation, the sticky bit is represented by the value 1 in the thousands place. For example,

```
chmod 1777 /tmp
```

will set the sticky bit along with read, write, and execute permissions for all users. When the sticky bit is set on a directory, the t character replaces the x in the others' execute permission slot when displayed with `ls -l`. For example, `drwxrwxrwt` indicates that the sticky bit is set along with read, write, and execute permissions for all users.

It's important to use special permissions judiciously, as they can have security implications if not configured properly. Setuid and setgid executables should be carefully audited to ensure they don't introduce vulnerabilities that could allow regular users to gain unintended privileges. The find command, which we covered in an earlier chapter, can be used to locate files with specific permissions, including special permissions. For example,

```
find / -perm /4000
```

will search the entire filesystem for files with the setuid bit set.

```
find / -perm /2000
```

will search for files with the setgid bit set, and

```
find / -perm /1000
```

will search for directories with the sticky bit set. The / before the permission value in these examples means "any of the specified bits are set." You can also search for files with exact permission matches. For example,

```
find /usr/bin -perm 4755
```

will search for files in /usr/bin with the exact permissions 4755 (setuid, owner rwx, group rx, others rx).

The umask command is used to control the default file permissions assigned to newly created files and directories. umask stands for "user file-creation mode mask." It's a bitmask that specifies which permissions should be masked out (disabled) when a file or directory is created. The umask value is typically set in the user's shell configuration files, such as ~/.bashrc or ~/.bash_profile. The default umask value on many systems is 0022, which results in files being created with permissions 644 (rw-r--r--) and directories being created with permissions 755 (rwxr-xr-x).

When a file is created, the system starts with a default permission of 666 (rw-rw-rw-) for regular files and 777 (rwxrwxrwx) for directories. The umask value is then subtracted from these default permissions to determine the final permissions. For example, with a umask of 0022, when a regular file is created, the system starts with 666 (rw-rw-rw-) and subtracts 022, resulting in 644 (rw-r--r--). When a directory is created, the system starts with 777 (rwxrwxrwx) and subtracts 022, resulting in 755 (rwxr-xr-x).

To view the current umask value, you can simply run

```
umask
```

without any arguments. To set a new umask value, you can use

```
umask newvalue
```

, where "newvalue" is the desired umask value in octal notation. For example,

```
umask 0027
```

will set the umask to 0027, which will result in files being created with permissions 640 (rw-r--) and directories being created with permissions 750 (rwxr-x).

It's important to choose an appropriate umask value based on the desired balance between security and usability. A more restrictive umask can enhance security by limiting default permissions, but it may also require more frequent use of chmod to grant necessary permissions. Conversely, a more permissive umask can be more convenient but may increase the risk of unintended access to files. File Access Control Lists (ACLs) provide a more fine-grained mechanism for managing permissions beyond the traditional owner-group-others model.

ACLs allow you to specify permissions for additional users and groups beyond the owning user and group. They can be useful in scenarios where you need to grant specific permissions to multiple users or groups without changing the primary ownership or group of a file or directory. The `setfacl` command is used to set ACLs, and the `getfacl` command is used to view ACLs. For example,

```
setfacl -m u:jane:rx myfile.txt
```

will grant read and execute permissions to the user "jane" on "myfile.txt", in addition to the regular permissions.

```
setfacl -m g:sales:rw mydir
```

will grant read and write permissions to the group "sales" on "mydir". To remove an ACL entry, you can use the `-x` option. For example,

```
setfacl -x u:jane myfile.txt
```

will remove the ACL entry for the user "jane" on "myfile.txt". To view the ACLs for a file or directory, you can use

```
getfacl myfile.txt
```

. The output will show the regular permissions as well as any additional ACL entries.

ACLs are stored as extended attributes of files and directories. Not all filesystems support ACLs, so you need to ensure that the filesystem you're using is mounted with ACL support enabled. ACLs provide a powerful way to manage complex permission scenarios, but they also add complexity to the permission model. It's important to carefully plan and document ACLs to ensure they are applied consistently and don't introduce unintended security risks.

These commands and concepts provide a comprehensive understanding of file permissions and ownership in Linux. Proper management of permissions and ownership is essential for maintaining a secure and well-organized system. By understanding how permissions are structured, how to interpret permission strings, and how to use `chmod` and `chown` to modify permissions and ownership, you can effectively control access to files and directories. The special permissions (setuid, setgid, and the sticky bit) provide advanced access control mechanisms for specific scenarios, such as allowing regular users to execute commands with elevated privileges or ensuring consistent group ownership in shared directories.

CHAPTER EIGHT: Process Management

This chapter explores the crucial topic of process management in Linux. Processes are the fundamental units of execution in an operating system, representing running instances of programs. Effective process management is essential for maintaining system stability, optimizing resource utilization, and troubleshooting performance issues. You'll learn how to view and monitor running processes, understand process states, and control processes using signals. We'll also cover how to manage process priorities, schedule tasks using cron and at, and explore tools for analyzing process behavior. By the end of this chapter, you'll have a solid understanding of how processes work in Linux and how to manage them effectively.

In Linux, a process is an instance of a running program. When you execute a program, the operating system creates a new process and allocates resources to it, such as memory, CPU time, and file handles. Each process has a unique process ID (PID), which is a numerical identifier used by the system to track and manage the process. Processes can be in various states, such as running, sleeping, waiting, or zombie. The operating system's scheduler determines which processes get to run on the CPU and for how long, based on their priority and resource requirements. Processes can also create child processes, forming a hierarchical relationship known as the process tree.

The `ps` command is one of the primary tools for viewing and monitoring processes in Linux. By default, `ps` displays the processes running in the current terminal session. The output shows the PID, terminal (TTY), CPU time used, and the command that launched the process. For example, running `ps` in a terminal might show output similar to:

```
PID TTY             TIME CMD
```

```
1234 pts/0      00:00:00 bash

5678 pts/0      00:00:00 ps
```

This output indicates that two processes are running in the current terminal: the bash shell (PID 1234) and the ps command itself (PID 5678). To view all processes running on the system, you can use the -e (or --every) option. This will display a list of all processes, regardless of which terminal they are associated with. The -f (or --full) option provides a more detailed output, including the user ID (UID), parent process ID (PPID), process state, start time, and the full command line. For example,

```
ps -ef
```

might show output similar to:

```
UID           PID   PPID  C STIME TTY
TIME CMD

root            1      0  0 Jan01 ?
00:00:01 /sbin/init

root         1234      1  0 Jan01 ?
00:00:00 /usr/sbin/sshd

john         5678   1234  0 10:00 pts/0
00:00:00 bash

john         9012   5678  0 11:30 pts/0
00:00:00 ps -ef
```

This output shows that the `init` process (PID 1) is the parent of all other processes, running as the root user. The `sshd` process (PID 1234) is also running as root. The user "john" has a bash shell (PID 5678) and is currently running the `ps -ef` command (PID 9012). The `ps` command has many other options for filtering and formatting the output. For example, you can use the `-u` option followed by a username to view only processes owned by that user. The `-p` option followed by a PID allows you to view information about a specific process.

The `top` command provides a dynamic, real-time view of the processes running on the system. It displays a continuously updating list of processes, sorted by CPU usage by default. The top part of the `top` output shows system-level information, such as the system uptime, load average, total number of tasks, CPU usage, and memory usage. The bottom part shows a list of processes, with columns for PID, user, CPU usage, memory usage, process state, and command. The `top` command is interactive and accepts various keyboard commands. For example, pressing k allows you to send a signal to a process, typically to terminate it.

Pressing r allows you to change the priority (nice value) of a process. Pressing u followed by a username filters the display to show only processes owned by that user. Pressing M sorts the processes by memory usage, while pressing P sorts them by CPU usage. Pressing h displays a help screen with a list of available commands. To exit `top`, you can press q. The `htop` command is an enhanced, interactive process viewer similar to `top`. It provides a more user-friendly interface with color output, mouse support, and additional features.

`htop` displays the same system-level information as `top` but in a more visually appealing way. It also shows a graphical representation of CPU and memory usage. The process list in `htop` is scrollable using the arrow keys or the mouse wheel. You can select a process by highlighting it and then use function keys to perform actions. For example, F9 sends a signal to the selected process, F7 and F8 change the process priority, and F6 allows you to sort the processes by different columns. `htop` also allows you to filter the process list by typing a search term.

The `pgrep` command is used to find the PIDs of processes based on their name or other attributes. The basic syntax is

```
pgrep pattern
```

, where "pattern" is the name or pattern you want to search for. For example,

```
pgrep firefox
```

will output the PIDs of all processes whose name matches "firefox". The `-l` option includes the process name in the output along with the PID. The `-u` option followed by a username allows you to search for processes owned by that user.

The `pidof` command is similar to `pgrep` but is used to find the PID of a program based on its exact name. The syntax is

```
pidof program_name
```

. For example,

```
pidof sshd
```

will output the PID of the `sshd` process. The `pstree` command displays the process tree, showing the hierarchical relationship between processes. The output shows the parent-child relationships between processes, with child processes indented under their parent. By default, `pstree` starts the tree from the `init` process (PID 1).

The `-p` option includes the PIDs in the output, and the `-u` option shows username transitions when a process is running under a different user than its parent. The `kill` command is used to send signals to processes. Signals are a form of inter-process communication that allows the operating system or other processes to notify a process of an event or request an action. The most common use of `kill` is to terminate a process. The basic syntax is

```
kill PID
```

, where "PID" is the process ID you want to send the signal to.

By default, `kill` sends the TERM signal (signal number 15), which requests that the process terminate gracefully. Some processes may ignore the TERM signal or may take some time to shut down. To force a process to terminate immediately, you can use the KILL signal (signal number 9) by specifying `-9` or `-KILL`. For example,

```
kill -9 1234
```

will immediately terminate the process with PID 1234. It's important to use the KILL signal with caution, as it doesn't allow the process to clean up or save its state, potentially leading to data loss or corruption.

There are many other signals besides TERM and KILL, each with its own purpose. For example, the HUP signal (signal number 1) is often used to request that a process reload its configuration files. The INT signal (signal number 2) is sent when you press Ctrl+C in a terminal and is typically used to interrupt a process. The `killall` command is similar to `kill` but allows you to send signals to processes based on their name instead of PID. The syntax is

```
killall process_name
```

. For example,

```
killall firefox
```

will send the default TERM signal to all processes named "firefox".

The −i option prompts for confirmation before sending the signal to each process. The −u option followed by a username allows you to send signals only to processes owned by that user. The −v option displays verbose output, showing the PID and signal sent for each process. The `nice` command is used to start a process with a specific priority. In Linux, process priority is represented by a "nice" value, which ranges from -20 (highest priority) to 19 (lowest priority). By default, processes are started with a nice value of 0.

The basic syntax is

```
nice -n nice_value command
```

, where "nice_value" is the desired nice value, and "command" is the command you want to execute. For example,

```
nice -n 10 firefox
```

will start the Firefox process with a nice value of 10, giving it a lower priority than processes with the default nice value. Only the root user can specify negative nice values to increase process priority. Regular users can only specify positive values to decrease priority. The `renice` command is used to change the nice value of an already running process.

The syntax is

```
renice -n new_nice_value -p PID
```

, where "new_nice_value" is the new nice value you want to set, and "PID" is the process ID you want to modify. For example,

```
renice -n 5 1234
```

will change the nice value of the process with PID 1234 to 5. Like with `nice`, only the root user can specify negative nice values to increase process priority. Regular users can only change the priority of their own processes and can only specify positive values to decrease priority.

The nohup command is used to run a command that will continue running even after you log out or close the terminal. By default, when you log out or close a terminal, any processes running in that terminal are sent the HUP signal, which typically causes them to terminate. nohup prevents this by ignoring the HUP signal and redirecting the standard output and standard error to a file called "nohup.out". The basic syntax is

```
nohup command &
```

, where "command" is the command you want to run, and the & at the end runs the command in the background.

For example,

```
nohup cp -r large_directory /backup &
```

will start a large file copy operation in the background and allow it to continue running even if you log out. The output of the cp command will be redirected to "nohup.out". The bg and fg commands are used to manage background and foreground processes in a shell. When you start a process in a terminal, it runs in the foreground by default, meaning it takes control of the terminal, and you can't enter any other commands until it finishes.

To run a process in the background, you can append & to the command. For example,

```
sleep 60 &
```

will start the sleep command in the background, allowing you to continue using the terminal. The shell will output the PID of the background process. If you have a process running in the foreground and want to move it to the background, you can first suspend it by pressing Ctrl+Z. This will stop the process and return you to the shell prompt. Then, you can use the bg command followed by the job ID to resume the process in the background.

The shell assigns job IDs to background processes, starting from 1. To view the list of background jobs, you can use the `jobs` command. For example, if you suspend the `sleep 60` command and then run `bg %1`, it will resume running in the background as job 1. To bring a background process to the foreground, you can use the `fg` command followed by the job ID. For example,

```
fg %1
```

will bring job 1 (the `sleep` command in this case) to the foreground.

The `at` command is used to schedule commands to be executed once at a specific time in the future. The basic syntax is

```
at time
```

, where "time" specifies when you want the command to run. You can specify the time in various formats, such as "now + 1 hour", "3:00 PM tomorrow", or "8:00 AM January 1". After running the `at` command, you will be presented with an `at>` prompt, where you can enter the commands you want to schedule.

Press Ctrl+D when you're done entering commands. For example, to schedule a command to run 5 minutes from now, you can run

```
at now + 5 minutes
```

and then enter the command at the `at>` prompt. The `at` command is useful for running one-time tasks at a specific time, such as shutting down the system or running a backup script. The `atq` command displays the list of pending `at` jobs, and the `atrm` command followed by a job ID allows you to remove a scheduled job.

The `cron` system is used to schedule commands or scripts to be executed periodically at fixed times, dates, or intervals. It's a powerful tool for automating recurring tasks, such as system maintenance, backups, or generating reports. The `cron` system consists of the `crond` daemon, which runs in the background and checks for scheduled tasks, and the `crontab` files, which contain the schedules and commands to be executed. Each user can have their own `crontab` file, and there's also a system-wide `crontab` file located at /etc/crontab.

To edit your `crontab` file, you can use the

```
crontab -e
```

command. This will open your `crontab` in the default text editor. Each line in a `crontab` file represents a separate cron job and consists of six fields separated by spaces: minute, hour, day of the month, month, day of the week, and the command to be executed. The first five fields specify the schedule, and the last field is the command. You can use numbers, ranges, lists, or the asterisk (*) wildcard to specify the schedule.

For example, a cron job entry like

```
0 0 * * * /usr/bin/backup.sh
```

will run the "/usr/bin/backup.sh" script every day at midnight (0 minutes past hour 0). An entry like

```
30 8 * * 1-5 /usr/bin/report.sh
```

will run the "/usr/bin/report.sh" script at 8:30 AM every weekday (Monday to Friday). An entry like

```
0 */4 * * * /usr/bin/check_updates.sh
```

will run the "/usr/bin/check_updates.sh" script every 4 hours. It's important to ensure that the commands or scripts specified in `crontab` files have the necessary permissions and are specified with absolute paths.

The `cron` system logs its activity to the system log, typically located at /var/log/syslog or /var/log/cron. You can monitor the log to ensure that your cron jobs are running as expected and to troubleshoot any issues. The systemd init system, used in many modern Linux distributions, provides a more advanced and flexible way to manage services and schedule tasks. systemd uses units to define various system resources, including services, timers, and targets. A service unit represents a background process or daemon, while a timer unit defines a schedule for activating a service or running a command.

systemd timers are an alternative to cron for scheduling recurring tasks. They offer more features, such as calendar-based scheduling, monotonic timers (based on time since boot), and the ability to trigger tasks based on system events. To create a systemd timer, you need to create two unit files: a service unit that defines the command or script to be executed, and a timer unit that defines the schedule. The service unit file typically has a .service extension and is placed in the /etc/systemd/system directory.

It specifies the command to be executed using the ExecStart directive. The timer unit file has a .timer extension and is also placed in /etc/systemd/system. It defines the schedule using directives like OnCalendar or OnBootSec. For example, to schedule a script to run every day at 6:00 AM, you can create a service unit file named "/etc/systemd/system/mybackup.service" with the following content:

```
[Unit]

Description=My Backup Service


[Service]

ExecStart=/usr/local/bin/mybackup.sh
```

And a timer unit file named
"/etc/systemd/system/mybackup.timer" with the following content:

```
[Unit]

Description=Run mybackup.sh daily


[Timer]

OnCalendar=*-*-* 6:00:00

Persistent=true


[Install]

WantedBy=timers.target
```

The `OnCalendar` directive specifies the schedule using a calendar expression. `Persistent=true` ensures that the timer is activated even if the system was powered off at the scheduled time. After creating the unit files, you need to enable and start the timer using the

```
systemctl enable mybackup.timer
```

and

```
systemctl start mybackup.timer
```

commands. To check the status of the timer, you can use

```
systemctl list-timers
```

. systemd provides a powerful and flexible way to manage processes and schedule tasks in modern Linux systems.

These commands and concepts provide a comprehensive understanding of process management in Linux. Effective process management is essential for maintaining system stability, optimizing resource utilization, and troubleshooting performance issues. By understanding how to view and monitor processes using tools like ps, top, and htop, you can gain insights into system activity and identify resource-intensive processes. The ability to control processes using signals, manage process priorities with nice and renice, and run processes in the background with nohup, bg, and fg allows you to manage system resources effectively.

Scheduling tasks using at and cron enables you to automate recurring tasks and perform system maintenance without manual intervention. The more advanced systemd timers provide a flexible alternative to cron for scheduling tasks based on calendar events or system events. As you continue to work with Linux, you'll find that process management is an integral part of system administration and daily usage. Whether you're monitoring system performance, troubleshooting issues, or automating tasks, these skills will be invaluable. The flexibility and power of the Linux process management tools allow you to have fine-grained control over the system and tailor it to your specific needs.

CHAPTER NINE: System Monitoring and Logging

This chapter explores the vital aspects of system monitoring and logging in Linux. Monitoring system activity and logs is essential for maintaining system health, identifying performance bottlenecks, troubleshooting issues, and detecting security incidents. You'll learn how to use various tools to monitor system resources, such as CPU, memory, disk I/O, and network usage. We'll also delve into the world of system logs, understanding the different types of logs, how they are generated, and how to analyze them effectively. Additionally, we'll cover tools for real-time monitoring, log management, and generating system reports. By the end of this chapter, you'll have a solid understanding of how to monitor a Linux system and interpret its logs.

In Linux, system monitoring involves tracking the utilization of various system resources to ensure optimal performance and identify potential issues. Several command-line tools are available for monitoring different aspects of the system. The `uptime` command provides a quick overview of the system's current status, including how long the system has been running, the number of users currently logged in, and the load average. The load average represents the average number of processes that are either in a runnable or uninterruptible state. It's displayed as three numbers, representing the load average over the past 1, 5, and 15 minutes.

The `vmstat` command provides information about system processes, memory, paging, block I/O, and CPU activity. It displays a summary of system statistics at a specified interval. For example,

```
vmstat 5
```

will display system statistics every 5 seconds. The output includes information about the number of processes waiting for run time, the amount of free and used memory, the amount of swap space used, the number of blocks read from and written to disk per second, and the percentage of CPU time spent in user mode, system mode, idle, and waiting for I/O.

The `iostat` command is used to monitor system input/output device loading by observing the time the devices are active in relation to their average transfer rates. It generates reports that can be used to change system configuration to better balance the input/output load between physical disks. The first report generated by `iostat` provides statistics since the system was last booted. Each subsequent report covers the time since the previous report. For example,

```
iostat -x 2
```

will display extended I/O statistics every 2 seconds. The output includes information about the average queue length, average wait time, service time, and utilization percentage for each device.

The `free` command displays the amount of free and used memory in the system. It shows the total amount of physical memory (RAM), the amount of memory currently in use, the amount of free memory, the amount of shared memory, the amount of memory used by buffers, and the amount of memory used for caching. The `-h` option displays the output in a human-readable format, using units like MB or GB. For example,

```
free -h
```

will display the memory usage in a human-readable format. It's important to understand that Linux uses free memory for disk caching to improve performance. The "available" memory value represents an estimate of how much memory is available for starting new applications, without swapping.

The `top` command, which we covered in the previous chapter, not only displays a dynamic list of processes but also provides a summary of system resource usage. The top part of the `top` output shows the load average, CPU usage, and memory usage. The CPU usage section displays the percentage of CPU time spent in user mode, system mode, nice, idle, waiting for I/O, hardware interrupts, software interrupts, and steal time (for virtual machines). The memory usage section shows the total, used, free, and available memory, as well as the amount of memory used for buffers and cache. The `top` command is interactive and allows you to sort the process list by various metrics, such as CPU usage or memory usage.

The `sar` (System Activity Reporter) command is a powerful tool for collecting, reporting, and saving system activity information. It can gather statistics about CPU usage, memory usage, disk I/O, network activity, and more. `sar` is part of the `sysstat` package, which needs to be installed separately on some distributions. The basic syntax is

```
sar -u interval count
```

, where "interval" is the time interval in seconds between reports, and "count" is the number of reports to generate. For example,

```
sar -u 5 10
```

will display CPU utilization statistics every 5 seconds, for a total of 10 reports.

`sar` can generate reports for various system resources using different options. For example, `-r` reports memory utilization, `-d` reports disk activity, `-n DEV` reports network interface activity, and `-b` reports I/O and transfer rate statistics. `sar` can also save the collected data to a file for later analysis using the `-o` option. The saved data can be viewed later using the `-f` option. For example,

```
sar -u 5 10 -o datafile
```

will collect CPU utilization data every 5 seconds for 10 intervals and save it to a file named "datafile". Later, you can view the data using

```
sar -f datafile
```

.

The nmon (Nigel's Monitor) command is an interactive system monitoring tool that displays performance data for various resources, including CPU, memory, disk, network, and more. It provides a comprehensive view of system activity in a single screen. nmon can be launched by simply running

```
nmon
```

in the terminal. The interface is interactive, and you can toggle different sections by pressing keys. For example, pressing c displays CPU utilization, m displays memory usage, d displays disk I/O, and n displays network activity. nmon can also capture data to a file for later analysis using the -f option.

The glances command is another interactive system monitoring tool that provides a comprehensive overview of system resources. It displays information about CPU, memory, load average, processes, network interfaces, disk I/O, file systems, and more, all in a single interface. glances can be launched by running

```
glances
```

in the terminal. The interface is color-coded, with different colors representing different levels of resource utilization. For example, green indicates normal usage, blue indicates caution, violet indicates warning, and red indicates critical. glances can also run in a client-server mode, allowing you to monitor remote systems.

The netstat command is used to display network connections, routing tables, interface statistics, masquerade connections, and multicast memberships. It's a versatile tool for monitoring network activity and troubleshooting network issues. The

```
netstat -a
```

command displays all active connections and listening ports. The −t option shows TCP connections, −u shows UDP connections, and −l shows listening sockets. The −n option displays numerical addresses instead of resolving hostnames, which can be faster. The −p option shows the PID and program name for each connection.

The ss command is a newer utility for investigating sockets and is considered a replacement for netstat. It can display more information than netstat and is generally faster. The syntax is similar to netstat. For example,

```
ss -a
```

displays all sockets,

```
ss -t
```

shows TCP sockets,

```
ss -u
```

shows UDP sockets, and

```
ss -l
```

shows listening sockets. The −n option displays numerical addresses, and the −p option shows the process using the socket. ss also has advanced filtering capabilities, allowing you to filter sockets based on state, address, port, and other criteria.

The tcpdump command is a powerful packet analyzer that allows you to capture and analyze network traffic. It intercepts and displays packets being transmitted or received over a network interface. tcpdump requires root privileges to run, as it needs to put the network interface into promiscuous mode to capture all packets. The basic syntax is

```
sudo tcpdump -i interface
```

, where "interface" is the name of the network interface you want to monitor. For example,

```
sudo tcpdump -i eth0
```

will capture packets on the "eth0" interface.

tcpdump can filter packets based on various criteria, such as source or destination IP address, port number, protocol, and more. For example,

```
sudo tcpdump -i eth0 port 80
```

will capture only packets on port 80 (HTTP) on the "eth0" interface.

```
sudo tcpdump -i eth0 src 192.168.1.10
```

will capture only packets originating from the IP address 192.168.1.10. tcpdump can also save captured packets to a file for later analysis using the -w option. The captured file can be read later using the -r option.

The lsof (list open files) command is used to display information about files that are open by processes. In Linux, everything is a file, including network sockets, pipes, and devices. lsof can be used to identify which process is using a specific file or network port. The basic syntax is

```
lsof
```

, which displays a list of all open files and the processes that opened them. The output includes information about the command, PID, user, file descriptor, file type, device, size, and the name of the file.

lsof can be used with various options to filter the output. For example,

```
lsof -i :80
```

will display information about processes using port 80.

```
lsof -u john
```

will display open files for the user "john".

```
lsof -p 1234
```

will display open files for the process with PID 1234.

```
lsof /path/to/file
```

will display information about processes that have the specified file open. lsof is a powerful tool for troubleshooting issues related to open files and network connections.

System logging is a crucial aspect of Linux system administration. Logs provide a record of system events, errors, warnings, and other important information. Analyzing logs can help you understand system behavior, troubleshoot issues, detect security incidents, and audit system activity. In Linux, the syslog protocol is traditionally used for system logging. The syslog daemon (syslogd or rsyslogd) is responsible for receiving log messages from various sources, such as the kernel, system services, and applications, and writing them to log files or forwarding them to other destinations.

syslog messages are typically stored in text files under the /var/log directory. Some common log files include /var/log/messages (general system messages), /var/log/syslog (system log), /var/log/auth.log (authentication-related messages), /var/log/kern.log (kernel messages), and /var/log/dmesg (kernel ring buffer). Each log message typically includes a timestamp, the hostname of the system that generated the message, the name of the process or application that generated the message, the PID of the process, and the message itself.

The rsyslog daemon, which is the default syslog implementation in many modern Linux distributions, provides a flexible and powerful way to manage log messages. It can filter messages based on various criteria, such as facility, severity, hostname, and content. It can also route messages to different destinations, such as local files, remote syslog servers, or databases. The configuration file for `rsyslog` is typically located at /etc/rsyslog.conf or /etc/rsyslog.d/*.conf. It uses a rule-based syntax to define how log messages should be handled.

The `journald` daemon is a modern logging system that is part of the `systemd` init system. It collects and stores log data in a binary format, providing several advantages over traditional syslog, such as structured logging, indexing, secure storage, and automatic log rotation. `journald` captures log messages from various sources, including the kernel, system services, and applications, and stores them in the journal. The `journalctl` command is used to query and view the logs stored by `journald`.

The basic syntax is

```
journalctl
```

, which displays all log entries in the journal. The output is similar to reading a log file, but it includes additional metadata, such as timestamps with microsecond precision, user IDs, process IDs, and more. `journalctl` provides powerful filtering options to search and filter log entries. For example,

```
journalctl -u sshd.service
```

will display log entries for the SSH service.

```
journalctl -p err
```

will display log entries with a priority level of error or higher.

```
journalctl -k
```

will display kernel messages (similar to `dmesg`).

```
journalctl --since "2023-01-01" --until
"2023-01-02"
```

will display log entries between the specified dates.

```
journalctl -f
```

will follow the log in real-time, displaying new entries as they are added to the journal. `journalctl` can also export log entries in various formats, such as plain text, JSON, or CSV, using the `-o` option. The `logger` command is a simple utility for generating log messages from the command line or shell scripts. It sends messages to the `syslog` daemon or `journald`, which then handles them according to the configured logging rules.

The basic syntax is

```
logger message
```

, where "message" is the log message you want to generate. For example,

```
logger "This is a test log message."
```

will generate a log message with the specified text. The message will be tagged with the username of the user who ran the `logger` command and the PID of the `logger` process. `logger` can be used with various options to customize the log message. For example, the `-p` option allows you to specify the facility and priority of the message.

```
logger -p auth.info "User john logged in."
```

will generate an informational log message in the "auth" facility. The `-t` option allows you to specify a custom tag for the message.

```
logger -t myapp "Starting application."
```

will generate a log message tagged with "myapp". The `-f` option allows you to log the contents of a file.

```
logger -f /path/to/input.txt
```

will log each line of the specified file as a separate log message.

The `dmesg` command is used to display the kernel ring buffer messages. The kernel ring buffer is a fixed-size buffer in memory where the kernel stores log messages related to hardware, device drivers, and other low-level system events. When the buffer is full, new messages overwrite the oldest ones. The `dmesg` command displays the contents of the kernel ring buffer. The output includes messages generated during system boot and messages generated by the kernel while the system is running.

`dmesg` messages are useful for troubleshooting hardware and driver issues. They can provide information about device detection, initialization, errors, and other events. The `-H` option makes the output more human-readable by adding timestamps and color-coding. The `-T` option displays human-readable timestamps. The `-w` option follows the `dmesg` output in real-time, displaying new messages as they are added to the buffer. The `-k` option displays only kernel messages, while the `-u` option displays only userspace messages.

The `logrotate` utility is used to manage log files by automatically rotating, compressing, and deleting old log files. It's designed to simplify the administration of systems that generate large numbers of log files. `logrotate` is typically run as a daily cron job. It reads its configuration from the /etc/logrotate.conf file and the files in the /etc/logrotate.d directory. Each configuration file can specify options for one or more log files, such as how often to rotate the logs, how many old logs to keep, whether to compress rotated logs, and whether to create new empty log files after rotation.

For example, a configuration file for rotating Apache web server logs might look like this:

```
/var/log/apache2/*.log {

    daily

    rotate 7

    compress

    delaycompress

    missingok

    notifempty

    create 640 root adm

    sharedscripts

    postrotate

        /etc/init.d/apache2 reload >
/dev/null

    endscript

}
```

This configuration specifies that log files matching the pattern /var/log/apache2/*.log should be rotated daily, that 7 rotated logs should be kept, that rotated logs should be compressed (except for the most recently rotated log, due to delaycompress), that logrotate should not issue an error if a log file is missing (missingok), that it should not rotate the log if it's empty (notifempty), that new log files should be created with permissions 640 and owned by root:adm, that scripts between postrotate and endscript should be executed after log rotation (in this case, reloading the Apache configuration), and that the `postrotate` script should be run only once per log file, even if multiple logs match the pattern (`sharedscripts`).

`logrotate` is a powerful tool for managing log files and preventing them from consuming too much disk space. It's highly configurable and can be tailored to the specific needs of each system and application. These commands and concepts provide a comprehensive understanding of system monitoring and logging in Linux. By mastering these tools and techniques, you can effectively monitor system resource utilization, analyze system behavior, troubleshoot issues, and maintain system security.

Regularly monitoring system resources using tools like `uptime`, `vmstat`, `iostat`, `free`, `top`, `sar`, `nmon`, and `glances` allows you to identify performance bottlenecks, resource exhaustion, and other potential issues. Monitoring network activity using tools like `netstat`, `ss`, `tcpdump`, and `lsof` helps you understand network traffic patterns, troubleshoot connectivity problems, and detect suspicious activity. System logs, managed by `syslog` or `journald`, provide a wealth of information about system events, errors, and warnings.

Analyzing logs using tools like `journalctl`, `logger`, and `dmesg` allows you to diagnose problems, audit system activity, and detect security incidents. Log management tools like `logrotate` help you automate the process of rotating, compressing, and deleting old log files, preventing them from consuming excessive disk space. As you continue to work with Linux, you'll find that system monitoring and logging are essential skills for system administrators, developers, and power users. By incorporating these practices into your daily workflow, you can proactively identify and address issues, optimize system performance, and maintain a secure and stable Linux environment. The flexibility and power of the Linux monitoring and logging tools provide you with deep insights into the system's inner workings and enable you to tailor the system to your specific needs.

CHAPTER TEN: Package Management with APT

Package management is an essential aspect of using Linux distributions, ensuring that software installation, updates, and removal are handled efficiently. The Advanced Package Tool, or APT, is a powerful package management system used primarily by Debian-based distributions like Ubuntu. It manages software installation and maintenance, resolving dependencies automatically and providing an easy way to keep systems up-to-date. In this chapter, we'll explore how to use APT for common package management tasks, focusing on its command-line utilities, such as `apt`, `apt-get`, and `apt-cache`.

APT simplifies the process of installing software by automating the retrieval and installation of packages from software repositories. The repositories are collections of packages maintained and hosted by the distribution or third-party maintainers. APT handles dependency resolution, ensuring all required software components are present when installing new programs. This system contrasts with manually downloading and installing software, which often leads to "dependency hell"—the frustration of tracking down and installing numerous required packages manually.

Before installing or upgrading packages, it's good practice to update the package index files to obtain the latest package information. This ensures your system clears any outdated data and recognizes the newest available updates. You can do this with the `<pre><code>sudo apt update</code></pre>` command. By executing it, your system contacts configured repositories and updates the package database with the latest versions. It's worthwhile to run this command regularly, especially before initiating any install or upgrade actions, to keep the system synchronized with repository changes.

Installing new software using APT is straightforward. The basic command is `sudo apt install package_name`, replacing "package_name" with the desired software's name. For example, `sudo apt install vim` installs the Vim text editor. APT handles dependencies automatically, ensuring all necessary packages are downloaded and installed alongside your chosen software. If you want to install multiple packages, you can list them separated by spaces, like `sudo apt install package1 package2`.

Similarly, removing a package is effortless with APT. Use `sudo apt remove package_name`, substituting "package_name" with the application you want to uninstall. This command removes the specified package but leaves configuration files untouched. If you wish to remove both the package and its configuration files, opt for `sudo apt purge package_name`. Remember, APT only manages software installed via the package manager, so it does not affect manually installed applications.

Occasionally, when removing packages, you may leave behind dependencies that are no longer needed. To clean up such packages, use the `sudo apt autoremove` command. This tool scans your system, identifies, and removes orphaned or unnecessary packages lingering from previous installations. Regularly running this command helps keep your system clutter-free and avoids wasting disk space on unused software components. It's a simple yet effective way to maintain hygiene in your system package ecosystem.

To upgrade existing software to the latest available versions, use the `sudo apt upgrade` command. This command updates all installed packages to their newest versions, as outlined in the updated package index. If some conflicting upgrades require manual intervention, you may need `<pre><code>sudo apt dist-upgrade</code></pre>`, which handles these conflicts and can sometimes perform more comprehensive upgrades, including kernel updates. Both commands ensure your system benefits from the latest features, performance improvements, and security patches.

Sometimes you may want only to verify if updates are available without actually applying them. Use the `<pre><code>apt list --upgradable</code></pre>` command to preview all available package updates. This command lists the currently available updates for your installed packages, giving you insight into what requires attention without committing any changes to your system. Such a check is helpful when planning updates around your tasks, ensuring minimal disruption during essential work hours.

The APT system includes the `apt-cache` utility, valuable for searching and displaying package information. To search for a package, use `<pre><code>apt-cache search keyword</code></pre>`, replacing "keyword" with the term relevant to your desired software. This command returns a list of packages that match your search term, offering a way to explore available software without browsing repositories manually. Additionally, for more detailed metadata about a specific package, use `<pre><code>apt-cache show package_name</code></pre>`.

Another noteworthy querying tool is `<pre><code>apt list</code></pre>`, which lists all available packages or those matching a specific search pattern. Appending the `--installed` option, like `<pre><code>apt list --installed</code></pre>`, provides a list of all installed packages on your system. Knowing which packages are installed can be particularly useful in debugging, replication environments, or confirming that an essential package is present. Leveraging these search and query functions empowers users to make informed package management decisions.

Package pinning with APT allows you to control package versions and priorities, providing stability in specific setups or testing environments. You can configure pinning by editing the /etc/apt/preferences file, specifying package priorities with a preferred version or repository target. For example, pinning can ensure a particular package remains at a known working version instead of automatically updating. This functionality can prevent unintended major changes in controlled environments while still permitting selective updates for other software.

For situations requiring custom repositories, you add them via a `.list` file in `/etc/apt/sources.list.d/`. This file specifies package sources, improving APT's capability through external or specialized repositories. You can manually edit these files or use add-apt-repository for easier management, as seen in `<pre><code>sudo add-apt-repository ppa:repository_name</code></pre>`. Custom repositories expand software availability beyond default sources, crucial for specialized software not included in official distribution repositories.

To audit and verify installed packages, you can use `<pre><code>dpkg --get-selections</code></pre>`, listing all packages and their statuses. This command integrates with APT as part of the Debian package handling, providing a comprehensive package inventory for auditing purposes. For systems requiring periodic reviews or migrations, this output helps document software footprint, policies, and settings, ensuring that environments can be consistently replicated or rolled back if needed. Such transparency is beneficial in complex environments or compliance-sensitive scenarios.

APT provides logs of package operations in /var/log/apt/history.log and /var/log/apt/term.log. These files catalog operations performed by APT, recording installation, removal, and upgrade actions. Reviewing these logs can be invaluable for system audits or troubleshooting package-related issues, providing context around modifications to installed software. Understanding APT logs aids in diagnosing issues or tracing back changes when unexpected behavior arises, making troubleshooting systematic and based on historical evidence.

Package management via APT involves understanding repository priorities through the APT preferences system. The concept of assigning priority numbers to packages, known as "Pin-Priority," allows users to control package versions, helping to ensure critical applications remain stable. Lower numbers mean less priority, and higher values indicate preference. It enables a detailed configuration for system administrators demanding precise version management. For instance, you can prevent unstable or experimental repository packages from ever defaulting over stable packages.

Managing broken dependencies sometimes requires extra intervention. In such cases, `apt` can automatically attempt fixing with `<pre><code>sudo apt install -f</code></pre>`. This repair function resolves broken dependencies by installing missing packages or suggesting removal of obstructing packages. Running this command can clear up broken package states, restoring normal package management operation, and improving overall stability and reliability on Debian-based systems.

Simplifying PPA management can be achieved with the `ppa-purge` tool, often used to revert dependencies installed from personal package archives (PPAs). By executing `<pre><code>sudo ppa-purge ppa:repository_name</code></pre>`, you remove the PPA's packages and downgrade them to official versions. This utility undoes repository-based changes effectively, restoring stability without significant manual intervention. It is a go-to solution for safely attempting application versions without permanently impacting the system's package state.

Accessing more precise control over the package installation process can be done with `aptitude`, a high-level interface to APT. Characterized by robust dependency handling and a flexible command-line mode, `aptitude` is often favored for en masse operations or sophisticated package scenarios. For example, `<pre><code>sudo aptitude install package_name</code></pre>`, offers interactive dependency resolution, appealing to users needing granular control over package operations, effortlessly integrating other package management tasks, and making it a valued component in any sysadmin's toolkit.

In summary, APT stands as a cornerstone of package management for Debian-based distros, offering powerful facilities to install, upgrade, and remove software efficiently. Coupling its flexibility with ease of use, it caters to beginners while providing depth for advanced users. Through its commands like `update`, `install`, `remove`, and beyond, APT ensures controlled software environments, operational scalability, and seamless management. Unlock its potential, and you'll find Linux systems running smoothly, backed by a robust, adaptable package management ecosystem§ion.

CHAPTER ELEVEN: Package Management with YUM/DNF

In the world of Linux, package management is a critical aspect that helps keep the system organized, optimized, and secure. Unlike APT, used primarily in Debian-based distributions, YUM (Yellowdog Updater, Modified) and its successor, DNF (Dandified YUM), are package management tools used in Red Hat-based distributions such as Red Hat Enterprise Linux, CentOS, and Fedora. These tools allow users to install, update, remove, and manage software packages, along with handling dependencies, security updates, and repository management.

YUM was developed to improve upon the limitations of earlier package managers like RPM (Red Hat Package Manager), which required users to manually resolve and install dependencies. YUM abstracts this process by automatically identifying and resolving these dependencies, allowing packages to be installed with minimal friction. It utilizes repositories, collections of RPM packages hosted on servers, to fetch and manage software. YUM simplifies software maintenance by ensuring users have access to the most current software versions.

DNF is the next-generation package manager, providing a faster and more robust solution than YUM. It resolves performance issues seen in YUM, offering a better package dependency resolution mechanism, improved performance, reduced memory usage, and a plugin framework for extensibility. Fedora and other distributions gradually adopted DNF as the default package manager, marking a significant evolution in package management with features that streamline system maintenance while preserving backward compatibility with legacy YUM commands.

Before installing new software, it's customary to update the package lists to ensure the system is aware of the latest versions available in the repositories. This can be achieved using the
```
<pre><code>sudo yum check-
```

update</code></pre> or <pre><code>sudo dnf check-update</code></pre> command. This process is akin to "apt update" in Debian-based distributions and ensures that all information about available packages and updates is current. Regularly performing this check is a good practice for maintaining a secure and up-to-date system environment.

When it comes to installing new packages, the process is quite intuitive with both YUM and DNF. Using YUM, you can execute <pre><code>sudo yum install package_name</code></pre>, while DNF users would run <pre><code>sudo dnf install package_name</code></pre>. Both commands evaluate dependencies and handle the installation seamlessly. For example, to install the "vim" text editor, you would run <pre><code>sudo dnf install vim</code></pre>. If multiple packages are desired, you can list them after the "install" command, like so: <pre><code>sudo dnf install package1 package2</code></pre>.

Removing installed software is equally straightforward. To remove a package with YUM, use <pre><code>sudo yum remove package_name</code></pre>, while with DNF, use <pre><code>sudo dnf remove package_name</code></pre>. It's important to note that this command removes the specified package but leaves behind its configuration files. If you wish to erase these files alongside the package, utilize the sudo dnf erase package_name command, though configurations tend to be left for possible future installations.

During the life of your system, dependencies or libraries may become obsolete if no actively used packages require them. To handle this, YUM and DNF both offer the autoremove function that identifies and removes such redundant packages. Use <pre><code>sudo yum autoremove</code></pre> or <pre><code>sudo dnf autoremove</code></pre> to clean up these unneeded packages, freeing up disk space and reducing clutter. It's a beneficial routine action to integrate into your system management practices.

Upgrading installed software to the latest versions is essential for optimal performance and security. Utilize `sudo yum update` or `sudo dnf upgrade` to upgrade all installed packages to their most recent versions available in repositories. These update commands assess current packages and dependencies, apply necessary updates, and ensure your system reaps the benefits of recent improvements and fixes. Staying proactive with updates is key to maintaining a secure and efficient system.

To preview potential updates without applying them, you may run `dnf list updates` or `yum list updates`. These commands will present a list of packages with available updates, offering you insight into planned versions before proceeding with installation. Such visibility is especially useful for planning around software updates, minimizing disruptions to productivity, or postponing non-essential updates in environments requiring high availability.

For more granular control and insight into package management, the `dnf` and `yum` utilities provide search functionality. Use `dnf search keyword` or `yum search keyword` to locate packages related to your search criteria. This functionality streamlines the exploration of available packages without requiring direct repository browsing. To access detailed information on a specific package, users can employ `dnf info package_name` to retrieve metadata, including descriptions, versions, and repository sources.

Repository management is a key component of package management. For custom or third-party repository configuration, users edit files in `/etc/yum.repos.d/`, following specific directives that identify repository URLs, enabled status, and priority levels. For instance, specialized software unavailable in default repositories can be accessed this way, particularly when managing cutting-edge or proprietary software. Both YUM and DNF support these configurations to extend their capabilities through external repositories.

DNF supports a plugin architecture, simplifying the process of extending core functionality through add-ons. Available plugins can be installed using `sudo dnf install dnf-plugins-core`. This facility provides versatile enhancements, enabling features such as version locking, security audits, and local installations not present in the out-of-the-box DNF experience. It's an adaptive framework that empowers users to tailor package management functionality by leveraging community-contributed plugins or developing bespoke solutions.

Logs and history commands are invaluable for tracking changes in software management. YUM users can review `/var/log/yum.log`, while DNF users rely on `dnf history`, which summarizes prior transactions, portraying activity like installations, updates, and removals. This information is vital when conducting system audits or diagnosing anomalies in software behavior, ensuring a comprehensive understanding of historical package management activities and helping guide solutions based on previous actions.

Package group management is another feature available through YUM and DNF, allowing users to install predefined sets of packages corresponding to a software suite or functional group. Commands like `dnf groupinstall "group_name"` facilitate the installation of these cohesive bundles, such as development tools or server configurations, streamlining the setup of specific environments. It's a practical way to ensure that all necessary components are installed in a coordinated and efficient manner.

In cases where terminal-based package management requires graphical support, tools like YUM Extender (Yumex) provide GUI interfaces. While YUM and DNF are primarily command-line tools, these GUI alternatives enable users transitioning from GUI-centric environments to harness package management capabilities with familiar visual interactions. They're particularly useful for users new to Linux who prefer navigating software installations and updates through clickable dialogues rather than command inputs.

Handling package downgrades, necessary for reverting to prior versions when updates lead to instability, is feasible through DNF. Execute `sudo dnf downgrade package_name` to return to an earlier version explicitly listed in enabled repositories. This is particularly useful when applied updates cause regressions or compatibility issues within scripts or applications relying on specific software versions. By offering downgrade abilities, DNF enhances system flexibility and user autonomy in managing software versions.

Ensuring system consistency between installations on different machines often entails exporting and replicating package states. YUM and DNF support command sequences that compare or replicate package lists, enabling admins to sustain homogeneity across environments. For instance, `dnf list installed > installed_packages.txt` exports a system's package list, while a simple `dnf install $(cat installed_packages.txt)` replicates the environment elsewhere. It's a crucial method for enforcing consistency across development, testing, and production systems.

Whether it's YUM's legacy support or DNF's blazing speeds and dynamic plugin support, these package managers transform and elevate efficient system software maintenance. Navigating their array of tools and features broadens Linux utilization in enterprise settings, driving efficiency through automated maintenance, enhanced control mechanisms, and comprehensive logging. By embracing these capabilities, system administrators are equipped to manage and maintain highly functional, resilient Linux environments that cater to evolving software and user demands.

CHAPTER TWELVE: Shell Scripting Basics

Shell scripting in Linux is a powerful way to automate tasks, streamline workflows, and perform complex sequences of operations with minimal intervention. It can help both beginners and advanced users to carry out routine tasks more efficiently, saving time and reducing errors. A shell script is a text file containing a sequence of commands for the shell to execute. The shell itself is a command-line interface that interprets user commands and manages their execution. This chapter delves into the basics of shell scripting, covering essential concepts and techniques that will enable you to create and manage your own scripts.

To get started with shell scripting, the first step is to understand what a shell script is and how it can be used. A shell script is essentially a script file that contains a list of commands you would normally type at the command line. When executed, these commands are run in sequence. This allows you to automate tasks, such as file manipulation, program execution, and printing text. Shell scripts can be used to perform simple jobs or even create complex programs by processing input and output, implementing logic flows, and manipulating data.

Before writing your first script, you'll need a text editor to compose your commands. Popular text editors like nano, vi, or gedit are suitable for writing shell scripts. Once you've opened your editor, begin your script with the shebang line:

```
#!/bin/bash
```

. This line, placed at the very top of your script, tells the system which shell should be used to interpret the script. In this case, "/bin/bash" signifies the use of the Bourne Again Shell, a common choice for scripting.

After the shebang line, you can begin writing your commands. For example, a simple script to display "Hello, World!" on the terminal would look like this:

. Save your script with a .sh extension, such as "hello.sh". To execute your script, you first need to make it executable using the chmod command:

!/bin/bash

```
echo "Hello, World!"
```

. Save your script with a .sh extension, such as "hello.sh". To execute your script, you first need to make it executable using the chmod command:

```
chmod +x hello.sh
```

. Then, you can run it by typing

```
./hello.sh
```

into the terminal.

Variables play a crucial role in shell scripting, allowing you to store and manipulate data dynamically. A variable is simply a named space in memory where you can store data. In shell scripting, variables are defined without the need for a data type. To create a variable, simply use the equal sign without spaces:

```
MYVAR="Hello"
```

. You can then reference this variable by prefixing it with the dollar sign:

```
echo $MYVAR
```

. This flexibility makes it easy to manage data and change script behavior according to your needs.

Arithmetic operations within shell scripts are straightforward, using tools like the expr command or double parentheses for arithmetic expansion. For example, you can calculate an expression using expr:

```
expr 5 + 3
```

, or you can use $((...)) for more readability:

```
result=$((5 + 3))
```

. These constructs support basic arithmetic operations such as addition, subtraction, multiplication, division, and modulus, making it easy to perform calculations as part of your scripting tasks.

Handling input and output efficiently is another fundamental aspect of shell scripting. You can use the read command to capture user input:

```
read name
```

will prompt the user to enter a name, which can be stored in a variable called 'name' for later use. Similarly, output can be managed using the echo command, as seen earlier. However, shell scripting also offers redirection operators, such as > to redirect output to a file or < to read input from a file.

Control structures, like loops and conditionals, enable you to make decisions and repeat actions within your scripts. The if statement lets you execute a command based on a condition. Its basic syntax is:

```
if [ condition ]; then
```

```
commands
```

```
fi
```

. For loops allow you to iterate through sequences or lists:

```
for i in 1 2 3; do

echo $i

done
```

. Similarly, while loops execute commands as long as a condition is true:

```
while [ condition ]; do

commands

done
```

.

Shell scripts can call functions, similar to other programming languages, for better organization and reuse of code blocks. A function in a shell script is defined with the following syntax:

```
my_function() {
```

```
commands
```

```
}
```

. You call the function by name within your script:

```
my_function
```

. Functions are handy for modularizing scripts and reducing repetition.

Comments in shell scripts, denoted by the hash symbol (#), make your code more readable and are used to explain sections or describe functionality. For example:

. Comments are crucial, especially in larger scripts, to clarify intentions and provide context, thereby aiding future updates and collaboration.

This is a comment

```
echo "This script demonstrates the use of
comments"
```

. Comments are crucial, especially in larger scripts, to clarify intentions and provide context, thereby aiding future updates and collaboration.

To handle command-line arguments, shell scripts use positional parameters. These are accessed within the script using $1, $2, and so on for each argument. For instance, a script to greet a user by name could look like this:

. Running

!/bin/bash

```
echo "Hello, $1!"
```

. Running

```
./greet.sh Alice
```

would output "Hello, Alice!", demonstrating the ease of incorporating user input at runtime.

Error handling and debugging can be managed using various techniques in shell scripting. Checking exit statuses is a common practice, represented by the $? variable. After any command's execution, $? holds its exit status. A status of 0 indicates success, while a non-zero value signifies an error. You can conditionally act based on these statuses to manage errors. Additionally, set -x and set +x can turn on/off debugging, providing a trace of executed commands within your script, which is invaluable for identifying issues.

Regular expressions can be used for pattern matching within shell scripts, significantly enhancing their text processing capabilities. The grep command, covered in earlier chapters, complements shell scripts well in tasks such as searching, replacing, or extracting data from files. For example,

```
grep "pattern"
```

can be incorporated into scripts to filter input data, making shell scripts adept at handling diverse data manipulation tasks.

Shell built-ins are commands integrated directly into the shell, offering efficient and convenient operation within scripts. Common built-ins include echo, read, and exit. Unlike external commands, built-ins execute faster since they don't spawn new processes. The help command provides a listing of available built-ins and a brief summary of their usage. Mastering shell built-ins can streamline script functionality and improve execution speed.

It's also essential to understand the environment variables and how they influence script execution. Environment variables, such as PATH, HOME, and USER, are predefined by the system and available to all script executions unless explicitly overridden. You can define your custom environment variables within scripts to control specific behaviors or store configuration details, enabling robust and versatile scripting solutions.

Lastly, file manipulation is a key component of shell scripting. Commands like cp, mv, and rm allow scripts to handle files and directories effectively. They can be used to automate backups, organize data, or manage system configurations. Combining these operations with control structures and conditionals provides vast opportunities for streamlining and optimizing complex workflows. Understanding how to leverage these capabilities is crucial to becoming proficient in Linux shell scripting.

CHAPTER THIRTEEN: Networking Fundamentals

Networking fundamentals are crucial for anyone exploring the Linux operating system, as they form the backbone of communication between devices. In Linux, understanding networking basics involves grasping how devices connect, communicate, and share data across different networks. We'll start by examining the essential components of a network infrastructure: hardware devices, software protocols, IP addressing, and data transmission methods. Mastering these elements enables anyone to set up, maintain, and troubleshoot Linux networks effectively.

A network is a collection of devices connected via physical or wireless connections to exchange data and resources. Typical network devices include computers, routers, switches, modems, and network interface cards (NICs). Routers connect different networks and manage data traffic, while switches link devices within a single network by forwarding packets. Modems convert digital data to analog for transmission over communication lines. NICs enable computers to connect to networks using wired or wireless mediums, ensuring seamless communication among devices.

Data communication in networks involves sending and receiving data packets between devices. Protocols guide this process by establishing rules for data exchange. The Internet Protocol (IP) suite, commonly referred to as TCP/IP, serves as the basis for most network communications. It consists of various protocols, such as Transmission Control Protocol (TCP) and User Datagram Protocol (UDP), that ensure reliable data transmission. TCP manages data packet organization and acknowledges successful packet delivery, while UDP transmits data without requiring acknowledgment.

IP addressing is an essential aspect of networking, providing unique identifiers for devices within a network. Two main types of

IP addressing are IPv4 and IPv6. IPv4 uses 32-bit addresses, typically expressed in decimal format as four numbers separated by periods. Conversely, IPv6 employs 128-bit addresses, represented by eight groups of hexadecimal numbers separated by colons. IPv6 addresses solve the address exhaustion problem prevalent in IPv4, offering almost limitless addressing for devices.

Subnetting is another critical concept in networking, involving the division of a network address space into smaller segments or subnets. Subnetting optimizes IP address allocation, reduces broadcast traffic, and improves network performance. Each subnet possesses a unique subnet mask, which identifies the network and host portions of an IP address. IPv4 subnet masks are often represented as a suffix, specifying the number of bits used for the network portion, such as /24.

Domain Name System (DNS) plays a pivotal role in networking by translating human-readable domain names into IP addresses. DNS functions like a phonebook for the internet, enabling users to access websites using easy-to-remember names instead of numerical IP addresses. Linux systems utilize DNS resolution through configuration files, such as /etc/resolv.conf, which contains DNS server addresses. Understanding DNS enables better troubleshooting and network management.

Network protocols facilitate communication by defining rules and conventions for data exchange. Besides TCP/IP, other notable protocols include Hypertext Transfer Protocol (HTTP), File Transfer Protocol (FTP), and Simple Mail Transfer Protocol (SMTP). HTTP governs data exchange between web browsers and servers, while FTP manages file transfers between devices. SMTP handles email transmission between mail servers. Recognizing these protocols enhances one's ability to manage data flow across Linux networks.

Network topology defines the arrangement and interaction of devices within a network. Physical topology refers to the actual device layout, while logical topology describes data transmission pathways. Common network topologies include bus, star, ring, and mesh. A bus topology connects devices in a linear sequence, while a star topology centers around a central hub. Ring topology forms a circular connection, and mesh topology offers multiple redundant paths. Each topology has its advantages and disadvantages, affecting network efficiency and reliability.

Firewalls serve as critical security devices in networking, controlling data flow between networks based on predefined policies. In Linux, firewalls filter network traffic to block unauthorized access, prevent data breaches, and protect sensitive information. Linux systems commonly use iptables and firewalld for firewall configurations. These tools enable users to define rules for data packets, specifying which traffic to allow, block, or redirect. Setting up and managing firewalls is fundamental to maintaining secure Linux network environments.

Network Address Translation (NAT) is a mechanism that modifies IP address information in data packet headers while routing packets between networks. NAT enables private IP addresses to communicate with public networks by translating internal addresses to external ones. This method conserves IP addresses and adds a layer of security by hiding internal network structures. Linux systems often implement NAT using iptables, allowing efficient configuration and monitoring of address translations.

Virtual Private Networks (VPNs) provide secure communication channels over public networks by encrypting data. VPNs protect data integrity and confidentiality, enabling safe remote access to resources. In Linux environments, VPNs are established using software solutions like OpenVPN or WireGuard. These tools create encrypted tunnels, making data packets indecipherable to unauthorized parties. Understanding VPNs allows users to set up secure connections between Linux systems and external networks.

Basic network troubleshooting is an indispensable skill for Linux users and administrators. Diagnosing network issues involves verifying connectivity, diagnosing IP conflicts, and assessing bandwidth usage. Tools like ping, traceroute, and netstat help identify connectivity problems by testing network paths and verifying device responsiveness. Command-line utilities such as ip, ifconfig, and route assist in examining IP configurations, addressing errors and modifying routing tables. Proficiency in these tools enables efficient detection and resolution of network-related issues.

Switches and hubs are network devices that impact data distribution and performance. Network switches efficiently direct data packets to specific devices using MAC addresses, reducing collision domains and ensuring optimal bandwidth usage. Hubs, in contrast, broadcast data packets to all connected devices, potentially leading to increased collisions and reduced network performance. Recognizing the differences between switches and hubs helps optimize Linux network design and manage traffic effectively.

Network cables play a crucial role in physical communications within networks. Common cable types include Ethernet, coaxial, and fiber-optic cables. Ethernet cables, often termed twisted-pair cables, connect devices using RJ45 connectors. Coaxial cables transmit television signals and data, while fiber-optic cables use light signals for high-speed data transmission across long distances. Familiarity with these cables aids in designing robust and efficient Linux network infrastructures.

Wireless networking has gained popularity due to its convenience and flexibility. Wireless networks use radio waves for data transmission, eliminating the need for cables. Wireless Access Points (WAPs) connect devices to networks within a certain coverage area. Wireless standards, such as Wi-Fi (IEEE 802.11), define data transmission protocols and frequencies. Linux systems support wireless networking through tools like iwconfig, which configure wireless interfaces, enabling seamless integration into Linux environments.

Network management involves the administration of network systems to ensure their performance, reliability, and security. Configuration management, monitoring, and automation are key elements of effective network management. Tools like Nagios,

Zabbix, and Prometheus offer monitoring solutions that track network health, detect anomalies, and generate alerts. Configuration management tools like Ansible and Puppet automate system configurations, reducing manual intervention and potential for errors. Implementing these practices helps optimize Linux network operations.

Routing is the process of determining the optimal path for data packets to travel from source to destination across networks. Routers play a critical role in directing traffic based on routing tables and algorithms. In Linux, routing is managed through commands like ip route. The concept of static and dynamic routing is fundamental, where static routing involves manually configuring paths, while dynamic routing uses protocols to adapt to network changes automatically. Understanding routing principles is essential for designing effective Linux network architectures.

Network performance monitoring focuses on evaluating the efficiency and reliability of data flow. It includes observing metrics like latency, throughput, and packet loss. Tools like iPerf and Wireshark analyze network performance by measuring data transfer rates and capturing packet information. Linux users can utilize these tools to identify performance bottlenecks, optimize data transmission, and improve resource allocation within networks. Effective performance monitoring enables proactive problem-solving and continuous network improvements.

Quality of Service (QoS) refers to the management of network resources to prioritize specific types of data, ensuring reliable delivery. QoS policies allocate bandwidth and assign priority levels to data packets based on their importance. In Linux, QoS is implemented using traffic control utilities like tc to manage network traffic efficiently. Enabling QoS helps maintain service quality for critical applications, such as video conferencing, by minimizing latency, jitter, and packet loss.

Understanding networking fundamentals in Linux empowers users to establish, maintain, and optimize network environments. By familiarizing themselves with key concepts like IP addressing, subnetting, DNS, and protocols, users gain the ability to work effectively with Linux networks. Combining this knowledge with practical skills, such as network troubleshooting, security configurations, and performance monitoring, enables Linux users and administrators to build resilient and efficient network systems tailored to their needs. The journey of exploring networking fundamentals fosters a deeper understanding of the Linux operating system and its capacities for connectivity, collaboration, and data management.

CHAPTER FOURTEEN: Configuring Network Interfaces

Configuring network interfaces is a fundamental skill in managing Linux systems, enabling them to communicate effectively over various networks. Network interfaces act as the gates through which a system connects to networks and exchanges data. Whether it's a wired Ethernet connection, a wireless Wi-Fi network, or a virtual interface, understanding how to configure and manage these interfaces is key to maintaining robust and efficient network communication for machines running Linux.

The first step in configuring a network interface in Linux is identifying the available interfaces on your system. This can be achieved using commands such as `ip link show` or `ifconfig`, which list all network interfaces and provide essential information like device name, MAC address, and current status. Network interfaces are usually named following a specific convention. For instance, `eth0` might represent the first Ethernet interface, whereas `wlan0` could signify a wireless interface. Understanding these identifiers is essential for subsequent configuration efforts.

Each network interface requires an IP address to participate in network communication. Assigning an IP address can be done manually or automatically through Dynamic Host Configuration Protocol (DHCP). Configuring a static IP address involves specifying the IP address, netmask, and gateway manually. This approach is preferable for servers or devices requiring consistent addresses. DHCP, on the other hand, dynamically allocates IP addresses from a pool, making it ideal for devices frequently moving between different networks, like laptops.

For systems using DHCP, the configuration process is largely automated. When the network interface starts, it sends a broadcast request seeking IP information. The DHCP server responds with a suitable IP address, subnet mask, gateway, and DNS details,

128

allowing the interface to configure itself automatically. Most Linux distributions integrate DHCP clients like `dhclient` or `NetworkManager` to simplify this process. Verifying DHCP configuration involves checking connectivity using `ping` or observing IP details with `ip a`.

Configuring a static IP address requires editing network configuration files. These files reside in different locations depending on your Linux distribution. In Debian-based systems, they are located in `/etc/network/interfaces`, while for Red Hat-based systems, you'd find them under `/etc/sysconfig/network-scripts/ifcfg-interface_name`. Manual configuration requires editing these files to include details such as the static IP address, netmask, gateway, and DNS settings, ensuring that these settings persist across reboots.

To ensure proper connectivity, adding a default gateway is crucial. The default gateway is the network point that acts as an exit point for traffic destined outside of the local network. It is typically the router providing access to external networks, such as the internet. In most Linux distributions, the default gateway is specified in the same configuration files as the IP address. When using static IP addresses, it's important to ensure that the gateway address does not conflict with other hosts on the network.

DNS (Domain Name System) configuration resolves hostnames to IP addresses. Specifying DNS servers is an integral step for making the network interface function correctly, as this ensures that applications can reach external resources via domain names rather than IP addresses. This configuration is typically done in the `/etc/resolv.conf` file or through network manager tools that automatically fill this file with DNS information obtained from a DHCP server or specified manually for static configurations.

Once network parameters are configured, it's essential to activate the network interface to confirm connectivity. Commands like `ip link set dev interface_name up` or `ifup` interface_name bring the interface online. Conversely, ip link set dev interface_name down or ifdown interface_name will deactivate it. Upon activation, you can test connectivity by pinging internal or external IP addresses and verifying that DNS resolution works, ensuring your configuration is functional.

Network interfaces can also be bridged or bonded to achieve specific network configurations. Bridging involves combining two or more network interfaces to act as one unified interface, facilitating communication across devices on different interfaces as though on the same LAN segment. Bonding, on the other hand, teams multiple interfaces to increase bandwidth or provide redundancy. Linux provides tools such as brctl and bonding driver modules to configure these complex setups, enhancing network reliability and performance.

In scenarios where multiple network profiles are required, tools like netplan (Ubuntu) or nmtui (NetworkManager Text User Interface) enable the easy switching between configurations. netplan uses YAML configuration files to manage network settings, whereas nmtui provides a convenient text-based GUI for managing connections. This flexibility is invaluable for users who frequently switch between different network environments, maintaining network configurations appropriate for each situation with ease.

Networking also extends to managing virtual network interfaces, particularly in virtualized environments or for creating isolated network segments on the same physical machine. Virtual interfaces, such as tap or bridge, allow the host system to connect virtual machines to the network or interconnect multiple VMs. These configurations can be achieved using scripts or virtualization tools like libvirt, which manage networking seamlessly alongside virtual machine operations.

Wi-Fi network configuration requires additional considerations compared to wired interfaces. Wireless networks, defined by

SSIDs, security keys, and authentication protocols, demand specific configurations. Tools like `wpa_supplicant` provide capabilities for establishing and managing Wi-Fi connections, allowing Linux systems to connect to secured wireless networks. NetworkManager is increasingly used for managing these connections across distribution platforms, offering a unified approach for both GUI and command-line users.

Performance optimization for network interfaces is another crucial aspect. Tweaking parameters like MTU (Maximum Transmission Unit) can significantly influence data transfer efficiency. MTU determines the largest packet size transmitted over a network. Incorrect MTU settings could lead to fragmentation, reducing performance; or oversized packets, causing transmission errors. Adjusting MTU settings requires experimenting with values that provide the best throughput without invoking fragmentation, tailored to specific network characteristics.

For expert-level management and monitoring of network interfaces, diagnostic tools such as `tcpdump`, `iftop`, and `netstat` offer insights into interface-specific traffic and connection statuses. These tools allow system administrators to capture packet data for analysis, monitor traffic flow, and verify the current state of active network connections. Leveraging such tools enables the identification and resolution of network issues, enhancing the reliability and security of network interfaces under management.

Understanding security implications is fundamental when configuring network interfaces. Administrators must ensure proper firewall rules are in place to protect the interface from unauthorized access. Employing iptables or firewalld establishes robust security policies. Additionally, using tools like SELinux or AppArmor can enable mandatory access control, providing extra layers of security and ensuring that the communication through network interfaces remains safeguarded against potential threats.

Lastly, network performance monitoring is supported by tools like `vnstat` or `collectd`, which provide historical data usage and interface statistics. Such monitoring solutions help detect usage patterns, bandwidth consumption, and performance bottlenecks. By analyzing trends and detailed historical data, users can anticipate requirements and optimize resources, ensuring network interfaces perform at their peak capacity over time, meeting the changing demands of applications and users alike.

CHAPTER FIFTEEN: SSH and Remote Access

SSH, which stands for Secure Shell, is a cryptographic network protocol that enables secure remote access to computers over an unsecured network. SSH is widely used in Linux environments to manage systems and transfer files securely. It provides a strong mechanism for authenticating users and encrypting data during communication, ensuring the confidentiality and integrity of transmitted information. Remote access has become a fundamental part of managing Linux systems, allowing administrators and users to control machines from virtually anywhere in the world.

To initiate an SSH connection, you need an SSH client on your local device, which connects to the SSH server on the remote machine. Most Linux distributions come pre-installed with the OpenSSH client, a widely-used SSH client implementation. The basic syntax for establishing an SSH connection is

```
ssh user@hostname
```

, where "user" is the username on the remote system, and "hostname" is its IP address or domain. Upon connecting, you'll be prompted to enter the user's password to authenticate and gain shell access.

SSH uses public-key cryptography to authenticate the remote computer and allow it to authenticate the user. When you log in for the first time to a remote machine using SSH, the client stores the server's public key in a `known_hosts` file, ensuring that future connections verify the server's identity. You can also use SSH keys for authentication instead of passwords. SSH keys offer a more secure and convenient method by generating a pair of keys — a private key kept secret and a public key that you upload to the server.

To create an SSH key pair, use the `ssh-keygen` command, which generates a private and public key. You'll be prompted to choose a filename and a passphrase for added security. By default, keys are stored in the `~/.ssh` directory. Next, you'll upload the public key (`id_rsa.pub`) to the remote server with the `ssh-copy-id` command, which copies your public key to the server's `~/.ssh/authorized_keys` file. This setup allows you to authenticate using your private key without entering a password for every connection.

Configuring SSH is straightforward, typically involving the server's configuration file located at `/etc/ssh/sshd_config`. This file allows you to change the SSH port, root login permissions, and authentication methods, among other settings. It's wise to change the default SSH port from 22 to an alternative. This minimizes automated attacks targeting the default port. After making changes, restart the SSH service with `systemctl restart sshd` to apply your configurations.

For enhanced security, you may want to disable root login over SSH. This prevents direct access to the system as the root user, reducing the risk of unauthorized modifications. To disable root login, find the line `PermitRootLogin yes` in the `sshd_config` file and change it to `PermitRootLogin no`. Additionally, using complex passwords and SSH keys further secures your system from unauthorized access, especially when exposed to the internet.

SSH allows tunnel creation that secures connections for other protocols. An SSH tunnel routes traffic from a local machine, through a secure SSH connection, to a specified endpoint. This method is useful for encrypting unencrypted protocols or bypassing firewall restrictions. Creating an SSH tunnel involves using the `-L` option with SSH, like this:

```
ssh -L local_port:localhost:remote_port
user@hostname
```

. With this setup, connections to the local port forward to the remote host's corresponding port securely.

In addition to establishing secure connections, SSH facilitates secure file transfers using tools like SCP (Secure Copy Protocol) and SFTP (SSH File Transfer Protocol). SCP allows you to transfer files between the local and remote machines efficiently. The basic SCP command syntax is

```
scp source_file
user@hostname:destination_directory
```

. Similarly, to retrieve a file from the remote machine to your local system, invert the source and destination paths.

SFTP, a secure alternative to FTP, provides an interactive interface for managing files on a remote system over SSH. To start an SFTP session, run

```
sftp user@hostname
```

. You can navigate directories, upload and download files, and manage permissions using familiar commands like `ls`, `cd`, `get`, `put`, and `chmod`. SFTP sessions utilize the same security and authentication mechanisms as SSH, ensuring secure file exchange across the network.

X11 forwarding is another SSH feature, enabling you to display GUI applications over a remote connection. By enabling X11 forwarding, you can run applications on the remote machine and view their user interfaces locally. To use this feature, add the `-X` option when establishing an SSH connection, like this:

```
ssh -X user@hostname
```

. Ensure the remote server allows X11 forwarding by setting `X11Forwarding yes` in the SSH configuration file. This feature enables seamless interaction with remote GUIs over a secure channel.

SSH also allows for port forwarding, which redirects a port from the local machine to a port on a remote server. This capability can be leveraged for various tasks, such as allowing secure remote desktop connections. To enable port forwarding, add the -R option in your SSH command to specify the local port, remote address, and port, like so:

```
ssh -R remote_port:localhost:local_port
user@hostname
```

. This setup tunnels connections from the specified remote port back to your local machine.

For environments requiring multiple simultaneous SSH connections, tools like tmux (Terminal Multiplexer) enhance remote session management. tmux allows you to create, detach, and reattach to terminal sessions, providing a convenient way to manage tasks between different windows and panes. By using tmux with SSH, you can maintain active sessions even if a disconnection occurs, rejoining your work unhindered without re-establishing your SSH connection.

To centralize SSH access management, consider using tools such as SSH keys manager or services like Ansible to handle keys across multiple servers. These solutions simplify deploying and updating keys efficiently, especially in large environments. Managing SSH access controls through these means mitigates human error, ensures timely rotation of keys, and tracks which keys belong to which users. This process fortifies security and fosters better administrative oversight.

An important aspect of SSH is maintaining strong security by regularly updating the OpenSSH software and reviewing logs for suspicious activity. Ensure your system receives updates by regularly updating your package management system. OpenSSH development continues to address vulnerabilities, underlining the necessity of staying current. Additionally, monitoring logs within /var/log/auth.log helps detect unauthorized access attempts and informs responsive action for securing your host in the event of anomalies.

Complementing SSH, alternative remote access tools like VNC (Virtual Network Computing) or Remote Desktop Protocol (RDP) provide graphical interfaces. Though differing from SSH's command-line nature, these tools cater to scenarios where GUI-based operations are preferred. VNC and RDP are useful for users interested in managing remote desktops with visual interfaces, allowing shared screen capabilities and proactive remote machine administration.

By mastering SSH and its extensive capabilities, you empower yourself to manage Linux systems efficiently and securely from virtually any location. Whether securing data transfers, managing servers, or establishing complex network tunnels, SSH is a crucial component of a robust Linux toolkit. Embracing its features and best practices enhances your ability to conduct operations remotely, facilitating the seamless integration of Linux environments into today's interconnected world.

CHAPTER SIXTEEN: Text Editors: Vi/Vim

Vi and Vim are two text editors that stand as cornerstones in the Linux ecosystem. Vi, short for "visual," is one of the oldest text editors and is available on almost every UNIX and Linux system, making it widely accessible and universally used. Vim, an acronym for "Vi IMproved," is an enhanced version of Vi, offering additional features and greater flexibility, making it the preferred choice for many users. Vi and Vim provide a powerful environment for text editing, allowing users to efficiently edit code, configurations, and other text files.

To begin using Vi or Vim, you'll first need to open a file. You can start Vi or Vim by typing

```
vi filename
```

or

```
vim filename
```

in the terminal, where "filename" is the file you wish to edit. If the file does not exist, these commands will create a new file. Upon launching, you will enter command mode, which is the default mode for both Vi and Vim. In command mode, keystrokes correspond to commands rather than text input, a distinguishing feature of these editors.

Understanding the modes in Vi and Vim is crucial, as they define how you interact with the editor. The three primary modes are command mode, insert mode, and visual mode. Command mode allows you to execute commands for navigation, editing, and managing files. Insert mode is where you can enter text. You can switch to insert mode by pressing 'i', 'a', or other insert commands, and you can return to command mode by pressing 'Esc'. Visual mode lets you select sections of text for highlighting, yank, or delete operations.

Navigating through a file efficiently is one of the core strengths of Vi and Vim. You can use the 'h', 'j', 'k', and 'l' keys to move left, down, up, and right, respectively. You can skip words with 'w' and 'b', jump to the start or end of a line with '0' and '$', or search for specific text using '/searchtext'. These keystrokes minimize the need for arrow keys or a mouse, speed up the workflow, and harness the keyboard's full potential.

Inserting and modifying text becomes seamless when you familiarize yourself with the relevant commands. Use 'i' to insert text before the cursor, 'a' to append text after the cursor, 'o' to open a new line below, and 'O' for a new line above. For deletion, 'x' removes the character under the cursor, 'dw' deletes a word, and 'dd' deletes a whole line. These commands allow you to precisely control how text is changed, giving you considerable editing power.

Copying and pasting, often referred to as "yanking" and "putting" in Vi and Vim, involves using commands like 'y' and 'p'. The 'yy' command yanks an entire line, and 'yw' yanks a word, storing it in a buffer. You can paste or put that text back with 'p' to insert it after the cursor or 'P' to insert before. Using visual mode, you can highlight sections and use 'y' to yank selected text, giving you versatility in text manipulation.

Undoing and redoing changes are straightforward in both editors. Press 'u' to undo the last change, or press 'Ctrl-r' to redo an undone change. This functionality allows you to experiment freely, knowing that it's easy to revert any undesired edits. Combine this with the '.t' command to repeat the last action, and you'll find yourself navigating through edits confidently and efficiently, minimizing potential errors as you refine your files.

Searching and replacing are simplified with powerful commands in Vi and Vim. To search for a term, enter '/pattern' to search forward or '?pattern' to search backward. You can navigate through matches with 'n' and 'N'. For search and replace, use ':s/search/replace/g' within a line or expand this to a range, like ':%s/search/replace/g', to modify every instance in the entire file. This feature enables quick and efficient text transformation across large documents.

Customizing your Vi or Vim experience through configuration files can enhance productivity. The '.vimrc' file located in your home directory configures Vim, enabling you to set options, define key mappings, or include plugins. For example, adding 'set number' shows line numbers, and 'syntax on' enables syntax highlighting. These adjustments can tailor the environment to suit your needs and streamline your workflow, making Vim more accessible and efficient.

Vi and Vim's robust set of plugins extend the functionality further, supporting tasks beyond text editing. From syntax checking and version control to enhanced navigation and language-specific features, plugins such as 'nerdtree' for file exploration or 'fugitive' for Git integration can be installed via plugin managers like 'Vundle' or 'Pathogen'. These tools allow you to customize Vim into an Integrated Development Environment (IDE), maximizing efficiency for coding tasks.

Mastering complex file operations, like opening multiple files, can significantly enhance productivity in Vi and Vim. Use ':e filename' to open a new file or ':tabe filename' to open it in a new tab. Split-screen features, invoked with ':split filename' for horizontal splits or ':vsplit filename' for vertical splits, allow viewing and editing across multiple file windows. Navigate between splits using 'Ctrl-w' followed by the arrow keys, optimizing simultaneous file management.

Tag navigation leverages Vim's capability to scan source code with ctags to generate a tag file. This file serves as an index of function, macro, and identifier locations. Once tags are generated, ':tag identifier' quickly jumps to their definition, making it an invaluable feature for developers working with large codebases.

Efficient tag navigation reduces the complexity of code browsing, aiding in understanding and editing source code efficiently.

Vi and Vim's capacity for recording and executing macros further empowers users by automating repetitive tasks. Start recording with 'q', perform the tasks, and stop with 'q'. Playback using '@' repeats the recorded actions. Specifying numbers before macros, like '5@q', executes the macro five times. This functionality eliminates tediousness in repetitive actions, making editing faster and reducing errors.

Visual highlighting is another powerful feature in Vim, facilitating effective text selection and manipulation. Press 'v' for character-wise selection, 'V' for line-wise selection, or 'Ctrl-v' for block selection. Using these modes, you can easily highlight and modify large portions of text, yanking, deleting, or even substituting selected areas, which not only simplifies editing but also enhances precision when handling complex documents.

Encoding support in Vim addresses the need to handle files in various character sets seamlessly. Vim supports UTF-8, Latin1, and other encodings, ensuring compatibility with different languages and systems. To view or set file encoding, use ':set encoding' commands. Correct encoding settings ensure that text renders accurately and preserves data integrity when interacting with diverse files, making Vim indispensable for multilingual environments.

Advanced features like diff mode empower Vim for file comparison tasks. Using 'vimdiff file1 file2', you can observe changes side-by-side with highlights. Navigation through differences using ']c' (next difference) and '[c' (previous difference) simplifies identifying discrepancies across versions, especially useful for code reviews and synchronizing files. Diff mode, combined with robust editing features, positions Vim as a comprehensive file management tool.

Contact with the Vim community can significantly enhance your learning and comfort with the editor. Numerous online forums, documentation, and resources provide guidance and solutions to common questions. Platforms like vim.org, GitHub repositories, and Stack Exchange host discussions and plugin repositories that facilitate deeper engagement with the community, ensuring that users can leverage collective knowledge and experiences to master Vim effectively.

Exploring Vi and Vim introduces an invaluable skill set indispensable for efficient text editing. Leveraging their full capabilities enhances productivity, from simple note-taking to complex programming tasks. Whether managing configuration files, crafting documents, or developing software, Vi and Vim provide flexibility, power, and dependability. With practice, your proficiency in these editors will grow, amplifying your efficiency and accomplishments in the Linux environment.

CHAPTER SEVENTEEN: Text Editors: Nano

Text editors are indispensable tools for anyone working with the Linux operating system. Among the many options available, Nano stands out as a simple and user-friendly editor, ideal for beginners and essential for everyday tasks. Unlike Vi and Vim, which have steep learning curves, Nano offers an intuitive interface, making text editing accessible to all users. In this chapter, we'll explore the basics of Nano, its features, how to navigate its environment, and how to effectively edit files with it.

Nano is typically pre-installed on many Linux distributions, making it readily available without the need for additional installations. You can launch Nano by typing the command

```
nano filename
```

in the terminal. If the specified file does not exist, Nano will create a new one when you save. Upon opening, you will find yourself in an editing interface with the file's contents displayed and a list of commonly used commands at the bottom of the screen.

One of Nano's main strengths is its ease of navigation. Movement around the text is accomplished using the arrow keys, allowing users to move character by character or line by line. For quicker navigation, you can use the `Ctrl` and `A` combination to jump to the beginning of a line, and `Ctrl` and `E` to move to the end. These shortcuts make it easy to traverse even lengthy documents efficiently, without needing to lift your hands from the home row of the keyboard.

Nano provides straightforward text editing capabilities, ideal for adjustments and modifications to text and code files. To enter text, simply type where the cursor is positioned. Deleting is similarly straightforward: the `Backspace` key removes the character before the cursor, while the `Delete` key eliminates the one under it. For more significant deletions, Ctrl and K cuts the entire line, making it easy to change larger sections of text.

Copying and pasting in Nano employs the cut and uncut method - akin to cut and paste. Set the beginning of a text selection by pressing Ctrl and ^, then use arrow keys to highlight the desired section. Cut the highlighted text using Ctrl and K. To paste it elsewhere, navigate to the target location and press Ctrl and U. This workflow is particularly efficient when moving or duplicating blocks of text within the same document.

Nano also supports incremental searching, which is convenient for locating specific text within a file. To search, press Ctrl and W followed by the search term. As you type, Nano will provide instant feedback by highlighting the closest match. To find the next occurrence of the search term, simply press Ctrl and W again or Alt and W without retyping the word. This feature is invaluable when working with large bodies of text.

Undoing and redoing changes is a simple affair in Nano, essential for correcting mistakes. Use the Alt-U command to undo the last change, with repeated commands stepping back through multiple changes. Conversely, Alt-E redoes previously undone actions. This capability allows users to experiment freely, knowing they can easily retract unwanted modifications or mistakes without losing progress or introducing instability into their documents.

Nano's interface provides a set of convenient commands, displayed at the bottom of the screen. These include saving and exiting, both of which are critical operations in any text editor. Save changes with Ctrl and O, initiating a prompt for filename confirmation if it's a new file. To exit Nano once editing is complete, use Ctrl and X. If unsaved changes exist, Nano will prompt you to either save or discard them, safeguarding your efforts against accidental loss.

For more complex editing, Nano supports text justification, which aligns text in well-defined patterns. Justification is particularly useful when formatting documentation or preparing content for presentation. To justify text, move the cursor to the line or paragraph, then press Ctrl and J. Nano will then realign the content according to the current justification settings. Pressing Ctrl and J again removes justification if adjustments are later refined.

Nano is not limited to text editing alone; it offers additional functionalities to streamline common tasks. For example, text can be wrapped to fit within the visible screen area, preventing horizontal scrolling. Wrap mode is toggled with the Ctrl and W key combination, enhancing readability without compromising the original formatting of the content. This feature is helpful for writers or programmers who need constant oversight of complex lines and lengthy code segments.

Despite its simplicity, Nano allows basic customization to tailor the editing environment to meet individual needs. Configuration options reside within the .nanorc startup file located in the user's home directory. By adding specific commands, users can enable syntax highlighting for various programming languages, define custom keybindings, or set display preferences like line numbers or smooth scrolling. This versatility enhances Nano's usability for different types of projects.

Among Nano's features, syntax highlighting stands out as particularly beneficial for developers editing source code. When enabled, it uses colors to distinguish between code elements like variables, functions, comments, and keywords. This feature decreases the likelihood of coding errors by improving readability and accelerating navigation through code bases. Syntax highlighting can be activated by specifying the appropriate rules within the .nanorc file for the languages of interest.

A popular use case for Nano involves editing system configuration files, a common task among Linux administrators and users customizing their environment. It's essential to open these files with superuser privileges to apply any changes successfully. This is done by prefacing the Nano command with sudo, as in

```
sudo nano /path/to/configfile
```

. Accessing files this way ensures that system configurations are editable without typical permission restrictions.

Having robust support for multiple file editing makes Nano versatile for real-world applications. You can open several files simultaneously by specifying them at the command line, like

```
nano file1 file2 file3
```

. Within Nano, use `Alt-` and the left arrow for the previous buffer or `Alt-` and the right arrow for the next buffer, easily navigating through open files. This capability facilitates handling interconnected or dependent files efficiently.

Line numbers are helpful when debugging code or referencing specific sections in text documents. Nano supports displaying line numbers in the left margin, enhancing the editor's utility for code editing or large text files. This feature is enabled with the `Alt-` and `Shift-#` command, toggling numbered lines on or off. Especially for users collaborating on projects, this addition simplifies coordinated edits and reviews by clearly indicating line references.

While Nano might seem basic compared to other editors, understanding its file recovery features is crucial when handling critical projects. In case of unexpected closures or system crashes, Nano creates backup files using the `AutoSave` feature. Restoring editorial progress involves locating the `.save` file corresponding to the affected document and renaming it appropriately, preserving continuity of development and ensuring minimal interruptions.

Working with different file encodings is another valuable aspect of Nano, especially relevant in multi-lingual or region-dependent projects. Supporting multiple character sets like UTF-8 or ISO-8859, Nano accommodates diverse text sources and guarantees accurate character representations. Checking or correcting the file encoding through command-line options like `nano` `-` and specifying the format ensures content accessibility and correct interpretation across platforms.

Taking advantage of Nano's support for regular expressions empowers users to conduct intricate search and replace operations. By invoking search with `Ctrl` and `W` followed by `Ctrl` and `R`, you can toggle regular expression mode on or off, tailoring searches to locate complex patterns seamlessly. Such capabilities enable precise content transformations, equipping users with methods to efficiently manage large text corpora or sophisticated edit operations.

An often-overlooked benefit of utilizing Nano is its accessibility and availability across environments. Virtually all Linux distributions come with Nano, providing users with a text editor without requiring additional setup. This makes it ideal for users who need to edit files across different machines or through remote connections like SSH, ensuring a consistent, familiar experience regardless of varying configurations and hardware capabilities.

The simplicity of Nano belies its true power as a versatile, robust text editor for those navigating the Linux ecosystem. Mastering Nano's commands and exploring its capabilities equips users to tackle a broad spectrum of tasks, from basic file editing to intricate programming projects. As one familiarizes oneself with Nano, it becomes less a simple editor and more an invaluable, dependable tool in the Linux user's toolkit.

CHAPTER EIGHTEEN: Introduction to System Administration

System administration in Linux involves managing and maintaining the overall health, performance, and security of the operating system. It includes tasks like managing users, installing software, configuring network services, and monitoring system resources. Understanding these key aspects of system administration is essential for anyone responsible for ensuring that Linux systems run smoothly and efficiently.

A central component of system administration is user management. User accounts must be thoughtfully created and maintained to ensure proper access control and system security. Administrators need to understand how to handle user creation, modification, and deletion processes. Properly configuring user permissions and group memberships is crucial to restrict access to sensitive information and system resources.

Besides managing users, system administrators are responsible for overseeing file systems and storage management. This involves configuring, mounting, and unmounting file systems, as well as monitoring disk usage and allocating storage efficiently. Tools like `df`, `du`, and `fdisk` help in managing these tasks, enabling administrators to efficiently organize and optimize system storage.

Software package management forms another vital aspect of system administration. This includes installing, updating, and removing software packages to ensure that applications and services are up-to-date and running optimally. Package management tools like `APT` and `YUM/DNF` simplify these processes by automatically handling dependencies, ensuring smooth software installations and updates.

System administrators also manage network configurations and services to ensure reliable connectivity and data exchange. This includes configuring IP addresses, managing network interfaces, setting up DNS, and configuring firewall rules. Tools such as `ifconfig`, `netstat`, and `iptables` are commonly used for these tasks, enabling administrators to maintain secure and efficient network environments.

Monitoring system performance is critical for identifying potential issues before they escalate. It involves tracking resource usage, diagnosing system bottlenecks, and maintaining logs to ensure stable performance. Tools like `top`, `vmstat`, and `journalctl` provide insights into CPU, memory, and disk usage, allowing administrators to make informed decisions regarding resource allocation and optimization.

Security management is a top priority in system administration to protect systems from unauthorized access, malware, and data breaches. Security practices include configuring firewalls, managing access controls, rotating passwords, and applying security patches. Regular audits and security scans help identify vulnerabilities, ensuring a proactive approach to maintaining a secure Linux environment.

Backup and recovery are critical processes that safeguard data against loss due to hardware failure, corruption, or accidental deletion. Administrators need to establish regular backup schedules and implement strategies to quickly restore data when needed. Tools like `rsync` and `tar` facilitate efficient backup and recovery processes, preserving data integrity and ensuring business continuity.

Automation plays a significant role in system administration by reducing repetitive tasks and minimizing human error. Scripts and automation tools, such as cron jobs or system management tools like Ansible, can efficiently manage routine tasks like backups, updates, and monitoring. Automation helps streamline administrative processes, allowing administrators to focus on more complex issues.

Another key aspect involves managing services and daemons, which are background processes providing various system functionalities. Tools like `systemctl` enable administrators to start, stop, and manage services, ensuring that essential daemons are running as required. Proper service management maintains system stability and guarantees that dependencies are correctly configured.

Effective system administration also includes managing system configuration files, which define how services and applications operate. Administrators edit these files to set parameters for software behavior, user preferences, and operational policies. Understanding the structure and significance of files in `/etc` and other configuration directories is essential for finely tuning system performance.

Remote administration is increasingly important in managing Linux systems spread across various locations. SSH provides secure remote access, enabling administrators to perform tasks without being physically present at the system's location. Additional tools like `Webmin` offer web-based interfaces for managing systems, providing flexibility and convenience in remote system administration.

Documentation and communication are integral to system administration, ensuring that processes are transparent and consistently followed. Administrators should develop and maintain comprehensive documentation to guide processes like deployment, troubleshooting, recovery, and improvements. Clear communication with stakeholders ensures that system goals align with business objectives and user needs.

Troubleshooting expertise is essential for system administrators, who must diagnose and resolve issues promptly. Developing a structured approach to troubleshooting involves gathering relevant information, analyzing logs, testing hypotheses, and implementing solutions. Proficiency with troubleshooting tools and techniques empowers administrators to maintain system reliability and availability.

A key responsibility for system administrators includes managing hardware resources, which involves configuring and maintaining physical components like CPUs, memory, and peripherals. Monitoring hardware health ensures that systems operate within optimal conditions, preventing failures and prolonging the system's lifespan. Timely upgrades and replacements help accommodate evolving requirements.

Performance tuning is another important task that focuses on optimizing system operations to enhance speed and efficiency. This involves adjusting system parameters, optimizing application configurations, and fine-tuning hardware settings. Performance tuning helps improve response times, maximize resource utilization, and deliver a smooth user experience.

Collaboration with other departments and teams is vital for effective system administration, ensuring that IT solutions align with organizational objectives. Administrators should work closely with development, security, and support teams to address any challenges and implement joint strategies. Fostering a collaborative environment facilitates knowledge sharing and strengthens overall IT capabilities.

Proactive planning and capacity management enable administrators to anticipate growth and future demands on IT infrastructure. By evaluating trends, predicting resource needs, and planning architectural changes, administrators ensure that systems can scale efficiently and support business objectives. This forward-thinking approach avoids bottlenecks and reduces operational disruptions.

To maintain proficiency, system administrators should pursue ongoing education and skill development. This includes staying updated with industry trends, exploring new technologies, and participating in training programs or certifications. A commitment to continuous learning equips administrators with the knowledge necessary to adapt to evolving challenges and enhance their expertise.

Ultimately, system administration forms the backbone of a stable and secure Linux environment. By mastering these concepts and responsibilities, administrators ensure that systems operate efficiently, securely, and effectively. Their efforts contribute to user satisfaction, business success, and the smooth functioning of Linux infrastructure, proving that competent system administration is indispensable to the digital age.

CHAPTER NINETEEN: Installing and Configuring a Web Server

Setting up a web server in Linux involves installing server software, configuring the necessary resources, and ensuring the setup is secure and efficient for serving web content. Linux is a popular choice for web hosting due to its stability, flexibility, and the variety of open-source web server solutions available. This chapter provides a comprehensive guide to installing and configuring a web server on a Linux machine, taking you through the steps of setting up one of the most used web servers in the industry—Apache HTTP Server.

The first step in establishing a web server is selecting and installing web server software. Apache HTTP Server, commonly known as Apache, is one of the most popular and widely used open-source web server software. Known for its reliability, robustness, and flexibility, it is available in nearly every Linux distribution's package repository. To install Apache on a Debian-based system, the `apt` package management tool is used, whereas `yum` or `dnf` is employed for Red Hat-based distributions. Use `sudo apt install apache2` or `sudo dnf install httpd` to install Apache on your system.

Once installed, it is crucial to start the Apache service to ensure the web server is running. Systemd, the system and service manager, controls services in most modern Linux distributions. You can start Apache with the command `sudo systemctl start apache2` for Debian-based systems or `sudo systemctl start httpd` for Red Hat-based systems. These commands initiate the Apache service, allowing your server to begin responding to incoming HTTP requests.

To ensure Apache starts automatically at system boot, enabling the service is a necessary step. By executing `sudo systemctl enable apache2` or `sudo systemctl enable httpd`, depending on your distribution, the service is set to start with the system, ensuring your web server is always available after reboots. Confirm the service's status with `sudo systemctl status apache2` or `sudo systemctl status httpd` to verify it's running and set to enable. Monitoring this status helps catch any startup issues early on.

After getting the Apache server running, confirming that it serves content correctly is crucial. Open a web browser and access your server by typing `http://localhost/` or `http://your_server_ip/`. If the installation is successful, you will see the default Apache welcome page, confirming that the server is operating correctly and can serve content. This default page is generally stored in the `/var/www/html` directory, where you can place additional files for serving online.

The Apache server configuration files reside primarily in the `/etc/apache2/` directory in Debian-based systems and `/etc/httpd/` in Red Hat-based distributions. The central configuration file is typically named `httpd.conf` or `apache2.conf`. Here, you configure server parameters, modify settings, and apply custom configurations. Understanding the directory and file structure, as well as the configuration directive options, is essential for effective server administration.

To serve custom content and manage multiple websites, you must configure Apache using virtual hosts. Virtual hosting allows you to run several websites on a single machine. Each site requires its configuration file often residing in `/etc/apache2/sites-available/` for Debian or `/etc/httpd/conf.d/` for Red Hat. Define these with specific directives such as `ServerName` for domain association or `DocumentRoot` pointing to the directory containing site content. Creating virtual hosts streamlines web server management and optimizes resource use.

After creating virtual host configurations, you must enable them through Apache. On Debian-based systems, use the `a2ensite` script, followed by the configuration file name, to integrate your virtual host into the active configuration. Conversely, on Red Hat-based systems, all configuration files in `/etc/httpd/conf.d/` are automatically included. Afterward, remember to reload the Apache service with `sudo systemctl reload apache2` or `sudo systemctl reload httpd` for the changes to take effect without interrupting ongoing connections.

Security configuration is a critical element when managing a web server. One approach is securing Apache using the `mod_ssl` module, which adds Secure Sockets Layer (SSL) and Transport Layer Security (TLS) support for encrypting HTTP traffic. Install this module with `sudo apt install libapache2-mod-ssl` or `sudo dnf install mod_ssl`, depending on your distribution. Post-installation, create and configure SSL certificates for your server to operate securely, ensuring client-server data exchanges are protected from interception.

Another measure for enhancing security is implementing a firewall to control traffic. Tools like `iptables`, `ufw`, or `firewalld` restrict access to open ports, ensuring only legitimate user connections reach your server. Configuring the firewall to allow port 80 for HTTP and port 443 for HTTPS ensures visitors can access your content while blocking unauthorized access attempts, aiding in maintaining a securer web server environment.

Monitoring the server's performance and logs is essential in maintaining a seamless and efficient web server operation. Access and error logs, typically located in `/var/log/apache2/` or `/var/log/httpd/`, provide insights into user activity, resource access, and potential errors. Regular log checks assist in identifying unusual patterns or detecting early warnings of server issues, enabling timely interventions to avoid disruptions.

Enhancing the server's performance involves tweaking configurations to better match server capabilities and traffic demands. Adjustments like enabling caching with `mod_cache`, optimizing connection settings, or configuring compression with `mod_deflate` reduce response times and bandwidth usage, boosting overall performance. These refinements result in a more responsive server, enhancing user experience and overall satisfaction.

Installing additional Apache modules extends the web server's capabilities and functionality. Modules such as `mod_rewrite` offer URL manipulation, while `mod_headers` allows customizing HTTP request and response headers. Understanding module functionality will enable administrators to tailor the web server to specific requirements, addressing unique needs more effectively. Available modules are generally listed in configuration files or accessible via package repositories.

Automating management tasks simplifies the administration of a web server, saving time and reducing manual intervention. Implementing shell scripts that regularly update the system, clear logs, or generate performance reports, combined with scheduling tools like `cron`, streamline routine maintenance tasks. Automation enhances reliability, minimizes the potential for human errors, and ensures that the server continues operating efficiently over time.

For web server administrators dealing with potentially large or sensitive data, configuring backup routines is indispensable. Tools like `rsync` enable secure, incremental backups of web data and configuration files. Regular backups provide recovery options, allowing the server to restore its state in the event of data loss, corruption, or hardware failure, ensuring sustained availability and minimizing disruptions to online services.

Continuous learning is vital for maintaining a robust web server setup, enhancing the server's efficiency, security, and capabilities. By staying updated with the latest improvements, security patches, and best practices, administrators can proactively enhance the server's capabilities and resilience, offering users better services and experiences. Engaging with the community through forums and official Apache documentation sharpens skills and fosters innovation.

In the broader context, understanding the essentials of installing and configuring a web server in a Linux environment builds a solid foundation for more advanced web hosting configurations and applications. With these skills, whether hosting personal projects or managing full-scale enterprise solutions, one can ensure reliable, secure, and efficient web operations, contributing to an ever-expanding, interconnected world.

CHAPTER TWENTY: Introduction to Databases

Databases are integral to managing and storing data efficiently, a necessity in modern computing environments. In Linux, mastering database management opens doors to handling vast datasets, executing complex queries, and building robust applications. Whether for web development, data analysis, or system administration, understanding databases enriches your toolkit significantly. In this chapter, we'll introduce basic database concepts, explore popular databases on Linux, and provide guidance on their setup and usage.

At the heart of any database is its capacity to store data in an organized manner, structured for efficient retrieval and manipulation. Databases are broadly categorized into relational and non-relational types, each with its operating principles. Relational databases like MySQL, PostgreSQL, and SQLite organize data into tables interconnected through relationships. These systems use structured query language (SQL) for database management, enabling precise control over data insertion, update, and retrieval.

Non-relational databases, often known as NoSQL databases, offer flexible data models that cater to unstructured and semi-structured data. MongoDB is a leading example, providing a document-oriented approach where data is stored in JSON-like formats. Such databases excel in scenarios involving hierarchical data, real-time analytics, and applications with rapidly changing requirements. Opting for a particular type often depends on the data structure, scalability needs, and application specifics.

Installing a database on Linux typically starts with selecting an appropriate database server and acquiring it through the system's package manager. For example, to install MySQL on a Debian-based system, you might use the command `<pre><code>sudo apt install mysql-server</code></pre>`, while for

Red Hat distributions, you'd use `<pre><code>sudo dnf install mysql-server</code></pre>`. Most installation processes include setting up a root user account with a password, securing it through initial configuration scripts.

PostgreSQL, another popular choice for relational databases, offers advanced data integrity features and extensive language support. To install PostgreSQL, similar commands apply: `<pre><code>sudo apt install postgresql</code></pre>` or `<pre><code>sudo dnf install postgresql</code></pre>`. These installations come with command-line clients like `psql` that facilitate database interactions through SQL commands directly. It's essential to initialize database clusters before usage, ensuring environments are ready for data storage and queries.

Integrating databases with applications involves configuring connections that allow transferring information between an application and its database seamlessly. Libraries or connectors specific to the programming language in use bridge this gap, translating commands from application logic to database instructions. Popular libraries include `MySQL Connector` for Python, `JDBC` for Java, and `SQLAlchemy` for object-relational mapping. Educating yourself about these connectors ensures seamless data-driven application development.

Database design plays a pivotal role in creating efficient systems. In relational databases, establishing a schema—defining tables, fields, and relationships—is vital for logical organization. Proper normalization, or structuring tables to reduce redundancy and enhance integrity, is crucial. For non-relational systems like MongoDB, understanding how data is organized, determining which attributes best fit documents, and designing collections effectively ensures advantageous performance and scalability gains.

Handling data through SQL introduces you to essential operations such as SELECT, INSERT, UPDATE, and DELETE. These operations are foundational, enabling you to manage data effectively. Queries allow data filtering, sorting, and aggregation, providing insightful interactions with databases. Advanced SQL features like `JOIN`, `INDEX`, and `TRANSACTION` ensure higher-level data manipulation and integrity control, allowing for complex, efficient query execution while reducing resource consumption.

Beyond CRUD operations, mastering database management involves understanding how to secure data, configure backups, and ensure performance optimization. Routine tasks include monitoring query performance, indexing heavily accessed columns for faster retrieval, and enforcing security measures like enabling SSL connections and assigning appropriate user permissions. Each of these strengthens reliability while safeguarding information, crucial considerations in data management contexts.

MongoDB's document-oriented model requires familiarization with its CRUD operations through methods like `insertOne`, `find`, `updateOne`, and `deleteMany`. Knowledge of aggregation pipelines—multi-step operations to transform and summarize data—is equally important. These applications enhance data access while enabling efficient data processing flows, providing diverse query capabilities tailored for evolving application ecosystems and datasets.

Understanding databases also involves platform-independent techniques, such as database migration—transferring data and upgrading schemas between environments. Tools such as `pg_dump` and `pg_restore` for PostgreSQL, `mongodump` and `mongorestore` for MongoDB, or third-party solutions like `Liquibase`, facilitate these transitions across systems. Mastering these techniques provides flexibility, allowing databases to adapt swiftly to technological and infrastructural shifts.

Replication and sharding strategies enhance database availability and scalability. Replication involves copying data across multiple servers, fostering redundancy that improves reliability and fault tolerance. Sharding partitions data across servers, boosting horizontal scalability and allowing databases to accommodate substantial data volumes. Understanding how to implement these strategies—considering factors like data distribution, network latency, and server configuration—is instrumental in optimizing database environments.

Securing databases involves multiple layers, starting with access control policies restricting who can perform operations within a database. Defining roles and permissions helps enforce such policies, ensuring only authorized users modify data or schemas. Encryption, both at rest and in transit, protects data from malicious interception during storage and transmission. Awareness of these practices cultivates an understanding of critical security aspects, essential to maintaining trust in data integrity and confidentiality.

Exploring database management tools can significantly streamline your database administration tasks. Graphical applications such as `pgAdmin`, `phpMyAdmin`, and `MongoDB Compass` provide user-friendly interfaces that simplify configuration, monitoring, and maintenance activities. Conversely, command-line tools like `mysql`, `psql`, and `mongo` offer advanced features adeptly supporting custom scripts and automation solutions. Familiarity with these utilities ensures diverse, practical methods for database management across varied operating conditions.

Database backup and recovery are critical processes ensuring business continuity despite disruptions or data loss. Creating backups through techniques like full or incremental dumps prevents catastrophic data loss, enabling restoration to previous states when needed. Scheduling regular backup routines using cron jobs or dedicated backup management software offers systematic protection, preserving data integrity and supporting uninterrupted operations.

Database performance tuning involves optimizing various system aspects to ensure peak responsiveness and efficiency. This can include indexing, query optimization, hardware resource allocation, and cache configuration. By refining these parameters, administrators can prevent bottlenecks, reduce query execution times, and enhance user interactions, leading to improved application performance and user satisfaction. Constant performance monitoring coupled with data-driven strategies inform necessary adjustments, aligning databases with dynamic operational demands.

Progressing from core database administration, exploring specialized areas such as data warehousing, analytics, and big data solutions can further broaden your database knowledge. Data warehouses centralize large data volumes, supporting advanced analytics and informed decision-making. NoSQL databases specialize in unstructured data analysis, processing vast datasets efficiently. Leveraging such advanced techniques unlocks complex insights, guiding strategic choices and growth trajectories in data-centric environments.

In summary, comprehending database fundamentals on Linux empowers users to adopt structured data management practices and build applications that harness data efficiently. Emphasizing relational and non-relational paradigms, installation procedures, secure configurations, and SOPs ensures a well-rounded understanding of diverse databases. Familiarity with these core concepts is instrumental as database technology evolves, keeping pace with emerging data needs, supporting effective decision-making processes across countless domains.

CHAPTER TWENTY-ONE: Security Basics

Understanding the basics of security in the Linux operating system is crucial for anyone from beginners to seasoned administrators. As Linux systems often host critical infrastructure in businesses, it's important to maintain robust security protocols to protect against both external and internal threats. Security encompasses various elements such as file permissions, user roles, network security, and system updates. By grasping these concepts, you can significantly enhance the security of your Linux environment.

Ensuring that only authorized users can access and modify files is a fundamental aspect of Linux security. This is primarily managed through a robust permissions model that governs read, write, and execute rights for files and directories. Each file on a Linux system has a set of permissions determining what actions users can perform. Understanding how to effectively manage these permissions using commands like `chmod` and `chown` ensures that sensitive information remains secure.

User management is another critical component in Linux security. Admins must create and manage user accounts carefully, assigning appropriate roles and permissions. They must maintain least privilege access policies, giving users only the necessary permissions they need to perform their jobs. By leveraging user and group functionalities, admins can segregate and control access, reducing the risk of unauthorized privilege escalation and potential system compromise.

Linux systems offer an array of tools for monitoring system access and logons. Managers can use tools such as `last`, `w`, and `who` to track user activities, logins, and logouts. These utilities provide insight into user behavior and identify unusual access patterns, which may indicate potential security breaches. By routinely monitoring these logs, you can react swiftly to any suspicious activity, further safeguarding your systems.

Another layer of security involves ensuring that your Linux system remains up-to-date with patches and updates, which often address newly discovered vulnerabilities. Regularly using package management systems like APT or YUM to perform updates keeps your system protected against identified threats. Remaining diligent with software updates is an easy but effective strategy to maintain a hardened defense against exploits and vulnerabilities.

Implementing firewalls is essential in preventing unauthorized access to network services. Linux provides powerful and flexible firewall solutions such as `iptables` and `firewalld`, which allow administrators to define rules based on incoming and outgoing traffic. Configuring these rules ensures that only legitimate network traffic reaches your system, effectively reducing the attack surface and enhancing network security.

SSH is widely used for secure remote administration on Linux machines. To strengthen SSH security, you should disable root login and use key-based authentication instead of passwords. Additionally, altering default SSH port numbers and employing SSH tunneling can further protect your system from unauthorized access. Configuring your SSH service with strategic security in mind significantly improves your defense posture against malicious actors.

Auditing tools can provide invaluable insights into system activities and security posture. Tools like Linux Audit Framework (auditd) capture detailed logs of system events and changes, offering comprehensive records for analysis. Utilizing these tools enables administrators to retrospectively analyze events, detect abnormalities, and enhance security protocols based on empirical data. Continuous auditing helps maintain vigilance and responsive threat management.

SELinux and AppArmor offer mandatory access controls (MAC) that provide an additional security layer, restricting processes' actions beyond the traditional discretionary access controls (DAC). These systems enforce policies that limit how applications interact with one another and with core system files. Configuring and maintaining MAC systems contribute to preventing software from being compromised and used maliciously.

Encryption is another essential element of security. Encrypting sensitive data both at rest and in transit protects against data theft. Linux systems can use various tools such as `gpg` for encrypting files and `openssh` for secure communications. By ensuring critical data is encrypted, administrators can safeguard information's privacy, ensuring that only those with legitimate keys or credentials can access the data.

Regularly checking for abnormal system behavior is intrinsic to maintaining Linux security. Enterprises should leverage intrusion detection systems such as Tripwire or AIDE to identify unauthorized changes to system files. These tools alert administrators to potential breaches, enabling them to respond quickly. Rapid detection and containment are vital components of an effective security strategy.

Physical security should not be overlooked. Securing the physical premises where servers are stored limits unauthorized access and potential tampering. Implementing surveillance, access controls, and installing server cages or lockboxes are measures that protect the hardware, supporting a comprehensive security framework that enforces a controlled environment for Linux systems.

Backup and disaster recovery planning are pivotal to maintaining security and ensuring business continuity. Implementing regular data backups and testing recovery procedures ensures that data integrity is maintained even after disruptions or breaches. Using tools like `rsync` for creating and synchronizing backup data maintains system readiness for unanticipated failures, minimizing potential losses and downtime.

Passwords remain a vital aspect of security strategies. Enforcing strong password policies and regularly rotating passwords ensure that account access remains controlled. Utilizing tools like `faillog` can help manage, monitor, and lock accounts following failed authentication attempts, reducing brute force attack vulnerabilities. Encourage multi-factor authentication where possible to enhance access controls further.

Staying informed about security threats and trends is crucial for swift adaptation. Subscribing to security bulletins and joining forums focused on Linux security allows administrators to remain aware of emerging vulnerabilities, patch updates, and shared expertise within the community. Staying engaged with industry developments prepares administrators to anticipate attacks and swiftly deploy countermeasures.

In fostering a culture of security within organizations, training and awareness play vital roles. Employees should be trained on security protocols, potential threats, and suspicious behavior indicators. Educating users about social engineering attacks and safe practices minimizes risks, ensuring that everyone contributes to maintaining a secure Linux environment.

Open communication channels between IT departments and organizational leadership support successful security initiatives. Regularly discussing security assessments, strategies, and projects ensures alignment with business goals and resource allocation. Visibility and understanding of security efforts create a supportive environment, fostering trust and collaboration across the organization.

Security basics in Linux build a robust foundation for more sophisticated security practices. By diligently applying these principles, you can protect your Linux systems, ensuring data confidentiality, integrity, and availability. This proactive approach safeguards not only the technical environment but also the business operations dependent on Linux infrastructure, allowing secure, effective, and resilient use.

CHAPTER TWENTY-TWO: Firewalls and Security Hardening

Effective firewall configuration and security hardening are crucial for maintaining robust defenses in Linux systems. Firewalls act as barriers between a trusted internal network and untrusted external networks, regulating the flow of data packets based on predetermined rules. Security hardening encompasses various strategies and measures to protect Linux systems from vulnerabilities, exploits, and unauthorized access. This chapter is dedicated to the essentials of configuring firewalls and applying security hardening techniques to ensure systems remain secure.

Linux offers several firewall solutions, each with its own nuances and capabilities. Iptables is a fundamental tool for configuring packet filtering rules to manage incoming and outgoing network traffic. As the primary firewall utility in many Linux systems, iptables operates by maintaining chains of rules organized into tables. Each chain corresponds to a particular operation, such as filtering, network address translation (NAT), or packet alteration. Through these chains, administrators can define rules specifying how packets should be handled based on headers, source, destination, and other criteria.

For users seeking a more modern and versatile solution, nftables provides an advanced firewall framework, taking over many functions traditionally performed by iptables. Nftables offers a unified syntax and enhanced performance, integrating seamlessly with various utilities while allowing configuration persistence through scripting. Its benefits include reduced complexity and improved scalability, making nftables a preferred choice for contemporary Linux distributions looking to optimize firewall management.

An additional firewall utility available in many Linux systems is firewalld, known for its straightforward interface and dynamic capabilities. Firewalld provides a simplified method for managing firewall configurations without service interruption. Utilizing zones, firewalld associates network interfaces with differing levels of trust, systematically regulating network traffic. Each zone has a unique set of pre-configured rules, allowing administrators to allocate specific protocols, services, and ports easily. Switching between zones makes adapting to diverse network environments quick and efficient.

Establishing basic firewall rules is a foundational aspect of system security, ensuring that only legitimate traffic is permitted. This involves defining restrictions on traffic flow between the system and potentially risky external addresses. Critical rules include permitting access to specific trusted IP addresses and services while blocking connections from suspicious sources. Tailoring firewall settings to reflect the system's functional requirements is imperative in establishing a robust, tailored security perimeter.

A common misconception when configuring firewalls is that permissible traffic is inherently secure. In reality, proper configuration requires careful consideration of potential attack vectors, focusing on both inbound and outbound traffic. Restricting outbound traffic is often overlooked, yet it is crucial for detecting compromised machines attempting to communicate back to malicious actors. Regularly auditing and updating rulesets help maintain effective defenses, adapting to evolving network landscapes and potential threat areas.

Firewalls are a powerful protection layer, but they must be part of a broader security strategy. Comprehensive security hardening ensures systems have resilient defenses even beyond network-based threats. Hardening involves a series of proactive measures to minimize vulnerabilities, including disabling unused services, securing access controls, and maintaining software updates. By reducing the attack surface of a system, hardening effectively decreases the likelihood that vulnerabilities will be exploited.

One key security hardening measure is implementing least privilege access policies, ensuring users have minimal permissions required to perform their tasks. Regularly reviewing user roles and permissions helps prevent privilege escalation attacks. Additionally, leveraging sudo to grant temporary administrative privileges enforces accountability, generating audit logs for all privileged activities. Enforcing strict password policies and utilizing multi-factor authentication methods provides further protection against unauthorized access.

System security is often compromised when unnecessary services run or remain accessible. Evaluating active services and disabling those not strictly required reduces potential entry points for attackers. Tools like systemctl and chkconfig allow administrators to manage the status and startup behavior of services efficiently. This proactive approach not only conserves system resources but also decreases the attack surface available to would-be intruders.

Another hardening strategy involves securing network configurations. This includes regularly reviewing active network interfaces and ensuring proper configurations, particularly concerning IP addresses and gateway settings. Using secure protocols, such as SSH for remote administration and secure file transfers, guards against data interception. Strictly controlling which machines can connect to networked systems provides another critical layer of protection afforded by vigilant network configuration management.

Data encryption is a vital component of any hardening strategy, ensuring the confidentiality and integrity of sensitive information. Encrypting files, directories, and filesystems protects data against unauthorized access and physical theft. Encryption tools, such as GnuPG and OpenSSL, offer versatile solutions for encrypting data at rest or securing communications. Implementing robust encryption practices is essential for compliance with privacy regulations and maintaining user trust.

In addition to software measures, hardware security should not be neglected. Physical access to systems can lead to unauthorized modifications and exploits. Measures such as securing server rooms, utilizing cable locks, and employing surveillance systems deter unauthorized physical access. Employing BIOS or UEFI passwords further protects systems by preventing unauthorized boot-level access, fortifying defenses against tampering attempts.

Monitoring and logging capabilities are crucial for detecting security incidents and responding promptly. Implementing logging with tools like rsyslog or syslog-ng offers continuous insight into system activities, enabling anomaly detection. Parsing and analyzing logs through automated systems can highlight deviations from expected behavior, aiding early detection of potential threats. Effective monitoring extends beyond system logs to application-specific logs, ensuring comprehensive coverage.

Engaging in regular vulnerability assessments and penetration testing identifies weaknesses in the system's defenses. These assessments simulate attack scenarios, providing insights into how potential attackers might exploit vulnerabilities. Conducted by qualified professionals or using automated tools, these assessments inform subsequent hardening strategies. Prompt corrective actions following assessments bolster resilience and enable continuous improvement within the security framework.

Security is a dynamic field, necessitating ongoing learning and adaptation. Staying informed about emerging threats, security trends, and best practices strengthens administrators' ability to anticipate and respond to novel challenges. Participating in security communities, attending training, and maintaining dialogue with peers fosters a culture of security awareness and innovation. By cultivating a dynamic security mindset, administrators ensure that systems remain protected against increasingly sophisticated adversaries. In deploying comprehensive firewalls and rigorously applying security hardening practices, administrators lay the foundation for a vigilant, robust defense posture. This holistic approach shields Linux systems from vulnerabilities and breaches, safeguarding both data and operational integrity.

CHAPTER TWENTY-THREE: Backup and Recovery

In the realm of computing, data integrity and availability are foundational aspects that can significantly impact both personal and professional environments. For Linux system administrators, understanding and implementing effective backup and recovery strategies is indispensable. Backup and recovery ensure that critical data remains safe and can be restored in the event of data loss due to accidental deletion, hardware failure, or other unforeseen disasters. This chapter introduces the tools and techniques necessary to establish robust backup and recovery systems on Linux, providing peace of mind and reliability.

The concept of backup is straightforward: it involves creating copies of data from your system so that it can be restored if the original data is lost or damaged. Backups can be conducted in various ways, from full system images to incremental snapshots that only capture changes since the last backup. A well-planned backup strategy considers factors such as data type, change frequency, and storage media. It's essential to determine which data is crucial and how frequently backups should be performed to ensure optimal protection with minimal resource use.

One popular tool for performing backups on Linux systems is rsync. It is a versatile utility that can synchronize files and directories between different locations with ease. rsync works by comparing the source and destination to determine changes, and then only transfers the necessary data. This makes it ideal for incremental backups. To use rsync for backup, you can run a command like:

```
rsync -av /source/directory /backup/directory
```

This command archives and synchronizes the contents of the source directory with the backup directory, ensuring the backup remains up-to-date with any changes.

For full system backups, which include the entire Linux file system, including the operating system, configuration files, and user data, tools such as `tar` and `dd` are commonly employed. `tar` can create compressed archive files that encapsulate directory structures. An example command for making a full backup with tar is:

```
tar -cvpzf fullbackup.tar.gz --exclude=/proc
--exclude=/tmp --exclude=/mnt --exclude=/sys
/
```

This command compresses the file system into a tarball while excluding dynamic directories like `/proc` and `/tmp` that are not necessary to back up. In contrast, `dd` can be used to create disk images by directly reading and writing raw disk data. It is typically used for making exact copies of storage media, a process known as disk cloning.

Storage for backups can reside on local devices or be distributed across remote locations and cloud-based solutions. Local storage involves using internal or external drives where the backup data is stored physically. This is often the simplest approach but poses risks should local hardware failure occur. Remote storage, such as transferring backups to a network-attached storage (NAS) or a cloud service, enhances resilience by safeguarding data off-site. The inclusion of cloud services like Amazon S3 or Google Cloud Storage provides scalable storage options that automate much of the backup management, though it requires reliable network connectivity for data transfers.

Automating backups is vital to maintaining consistent routines without manual intervention. `cron` jobs are often used to schedule scripts that initiate backups at specified intervals, ensuring that backups occur regularly. A simple `crontab` entry might look like this:

```
0 2 * * * /usr/bin/rsync -av
/source/directory /backup/directory
```

This schedule runs the `rsync` backup every day at 2 AM, minimizing disruption during busy hours and ensuring that data created or modified during the day is safely stored overnight.

Beyond the physical copying of data, backup management encompasses the verification of backup integrity. Regularly testing backups to ensure they can be restored correctly is an often-overlooked step that can spell the difference between success and disaster during recovery. Verifying involves restoring a backup to an isolated environment to confirm that all necessary files are present and functional. Only with successful testing can you trust that your backup strategy is reliable and capable of delivering data when required.

When disaster strikes, having a clear, well-documented recovery plan is indispensable. Recovery involves restoring data from backup sources back to the original or new system locations. It can be as simple as copying data back into place or as complex as fully automating the provisioning of a new server with all necessary configurations and data. Tools like `rsync` or `tar` make data restoration relatively straightforward; for large-scale recovery operations, configuration management tools such as `Ansible` can expedite the process by automating infrastructure provisioning alongside data restoration.

For those managing databases, backing up is slightly more complex, requiring specialized approaches to preserve active data. Tools such as `mysqldump` for MySQL or `pg_dump` for PostgreSQL create database dumps that capture the current state of the database. Automating these backups via scripts and cron jobs, complemented by transaction log backups for point-in-time recovery options, ensures consistent database preservation and rapid recovery in an outage scenario.

While backups and recovery plans focus primarily on data, they should be integrated into broader disaster recovery plans (DRPs).

A DRP outlines procedures for quickly restoring critical system operations after disruptions. This might include hardware repairs, data recovery, network reconfiguration, and even relocating operations in severe cases. A comprehensive DRP considers every component in the infrastructure and prioritizes services to restore based on business impact, offering a holistic approach to maintaining continuity.

To enhance disaster preparedness, consider routine disaster recovery drills. Conducting simulations of data loss scenarios validates your recovery processes and identifies gaps or bottlenecks within the plan. These exercises keep team members knowledgeable about response protocols, ensuring swift action during genuine incidents. Having a reviewed and rehearsed recovery procedure reduces downtime and mitigates adverse impacts on business operations.

Security of backup data is another crucial factor. Ensuring that your backups are protected against unauthorized access is vital. Encrypt backups, especially when storing them off-site or in the cloud. Tools like GPG (GNU Privacy Guard) can encrypt data at rest, ensuring only authorized parties can access it. Similarly, transport-level encryption like SSL/TLS should be employed when transferring backup data over networks, preventing interception by malicious actors.

It is important to note that an effective backup strategy includes data pruning. Without careful management, backups can consume substantial storage resources over time. Segmenting data by importance, setting retention policies, and adopting incremental backup strategies minimizes storage demands. Incorporating tools that perform deduplication further reduces redundancy by storing only unique data blocks, optimizing storage utilization and costs.

Furthermore, an often underappreciated aspect of backup management is understanding regulatory requirements related to data storage and retention. Depending on industry specifications, regulations like GDPR, HIPAA, or SOX may dictate how data is handled, stored, and accessed. Compliance isn't just a practice in due diligence but a legal requirement in many jurisdictions, underscoring the importance of integrating regulatory adherence directly into backup and recovery policies.

The rapidly changing nature of technology and evolving threats necessitates adapting backup and recovery tactics. Stay informed about new technologies, backup solutions, and best practices through continuous learning resources, online communities, industry publications, and professional groups. Engaging with others in the field encourages shared experiences, helping you to refine and innovate strategies, keeping pace with the ever-evolving digital landscape.

Adopting comprehensive backup and recovery strategies means creating a protective envelope for data, reducing risks, and enhancing resilience in the face of potential disruptions. By designing systems that balance efficiency, security, and reliability, you foster the continuous operations vital to organizational success, customer satisfaction, and peace of mind. Your ongoing dedication to safeguarding data becomes a pillar of operational excellence, upholding the high standards expected in today's digital world.

CHAPTER TWENTY-FOUR:
Troubleshooting Common Issues

Troubleshooting common issues in Linux is an essential skill that can greatly enhance your ability to work effectively within this powerful operating system. Many newcomers find the command-line interface and Linux-specific behavior somewhat intimidating, but once you are familiar with some common problems and their solutions, you'll find it straightforward to handle most issues that arise. As with any complex system, things will sometimes go wrong, but with the right approach and tools, you can often resolve these issues swiftly.

One of the first steps in troubleshooting a Linux system is to gather information about the problem. For example, if your system is behaving unexpectedly, you'll want to check the system logs for clues. Logs contain a wealth of information about system activity, including errors and warnings that can help identify the source of a problem. Use the `journalctl` command to view logs managed by `systemd`, or examine logs in the `/var/log/` directory for specific applications. Searching for keywords related to your problem within these logs can provide insight into what might be going wrong.

A frequent issue that users encounter is difficulty with network connectivity. If your computer can't connect to the internet or communicate with other devices, there are several checks you can perform. First, ensure that your network interface is up and configured correctly using commands like `ip a` or `nmcli`. Confirm that you have an appropriate IP address and that network cables, if applicable, are securely connected. For Wi-Fi networks, check the SSID and authentication credentials. If everything appears correct yet connectivity issues persist, try using `ping` to test basic connectivity with a known server or gateway.

Another common problem is software malfunction or unexpected behavior. If an application isn't working as expected, check if the package is fully compatible with your Linux distribution or kernel version. Some packages require specific versions of libraries, so use the package manager to verify dependencies. Additionally, ensure your system is up to date, as updates may resolve known bugs. If necessary, consider reinstalling the software. For applications that crash or freeze, start them from the terminal to see error messages printed directly to the console, which often help pinpoint the issue.

File permission issues can cause hindrances when trying to access or modify files. These issues often arise from misunderstanding who can read, write, or execute a file. Use `ls -l` to list permissions for files and directories and compare them against user and group associations. If permissions are too restrictive, adjust them with `chmod` or change ownership with `chown`. Avoid granting full permissions (777) unnecessarily, as this can create security risks. Instead, tailor permissions to provide just enough access for the required operations.

Disk space running out is another typical issue, leading to system warnings and application errors. Check current disk usage with the `df` command to identify which partitions are full. Use the `du` command to discover large files or directories consuming significant space. In many cases, clearing cache files, looking for old backups, or removing orphaned packages with `sudo apt autoremove` or `sudo dnf autoremove` can free up significant amounts of space. Managing log files is also important; use tools like `logrotate` to prevent logs from growing indefinitely.

Problems with the graphical display are also frequent among Linux users. If your desktop environment doesn't load or appears incorrectly, first ensure that your graphics drivers are correctly installed and configured. Use distro-specific tools to select the right drivers, as Linux often has both open-source and proprietary driver options. If you experience crashes, try booting into a different display manager, like by changing symbolic links for `/etc/X11/default-display-manager`, to see if an incompatibility exists with your current setup.

Boot issues can be daunting when your system doesn't start correctly or gets stuck during the boot process. If the GRUB bootloader fails, it's often due to configuration errors. You can reinstall GRUB from a live USB session if necessary. Kernel panics and module issues during boot need careful inspection of recent hardware or software changes. Boot into recovery mode or use a live distribution to repair your installation, adjusting configuration files such as `/etc/fstab` for misconfigured disk mount points.

With performance, various issues can cause systems to slow down intermittently or consistently. Investigating which applications consume the most CPU or memory using `top` or `htop` is the first step. Ensure that swap memory is available, as the lack of it can slow down systems under heavy loads. Inspect services starting at boot time to identify unnecessary ones that you can disable, saving resources for critical operations. Sometimes, kernel upgrades or different scheduling algorithms can help resolve deeper performance bottlenecks.

Missing configuration files can lead to non-functional applications or services failing to start. Verify that required files are in place by consulting program documentation for correct file paths and names. Sometimes configuration templates are included in a package but are not activated without manual copying or renaming steps. You can frequently find these under `*.example` or with similar naming conventions within `/usr/share/doc`.

Linux systems can sometimes behave erratically due to hardware issues, including failing hard drives or overheating components. Check the health of disk drives using `smartctl` for SMART data analysis and confirm temperatures with tools like `lm-sensors`. If cooling systems are inadequate, consider cleaning dust from within the chassis or renewing thermal paste to ensure efficient heat dissipation. If power issues cause random shutdowns, check power supply integrity and cable connections.

Software conflicts can be tricky to diagnose, particularly when multiple programs depend on conflicting versions of shared libraries. Verify consistency in installed libraries using package management system tools, and use version-specific installations where possible. Containerization using Docker provides an isolated environment to run applications with all their dependencies, reducing the chance of conflicts with system libraries.

One sometimes overlooked source of trouble is environmental variables. Many programs rely on these variables for finding resources such as files or executables. Misconfigured variables might direct programs to incorrect files or outdated versions. Use `echo $VARIABLE_NAME` to check their current settings and amend as needed within configuration files like `~/.bashrc`.

Linux systems are known for their stability, but they are not immune to security breaches. Regularly audit user accounts using the `getent passwd` command for entries without a valid login shell or requiring locked or expired passwords. SSH log files, typically found in `/var/log/auth.log`, are rich in information about unauthorized access attempts. In cases of suspected intrusion, isolate the system to prevent further damage and employ strategies such as rootkit detection tools, e.g., `chkrootkit` or `rkhunter`, for further investigation.

Kernel updates can also inadvertently introduce issues, especially if certain hardware components are not fully supported by new kernel versions. Retain older working kernels within the `/boot/` directory, allowing you to boot into them if necessary. It's advisable to only conduct kernel updates when required for new features or security patches, taking care to read through changelogs for potential impacts.

Finally, if custom scripts or services are not functioning, check for syntax errors, correct environment settings, and proper execution permissions. Examine relevant logs for clues, and if applicable, manually execute scripts or commands to isolate the problematic part of a larger automated process. Use shell-specific debugging options, like `bash -x script.sh`, to gain visibility into each execution step.

Understanding these troubleshooting strategies equips you with problem-solving techniques needed to navigate the complexities of Linux system management. Developing systematic investigation skills ensures you address problems efficiently and effectively, allowing you to maintain high system performance and reliability in any environment.

CHAPTER TWENTY-FIVE: Further Exploration and Resources

Diving into the Linux ecosystem opens up a vast world of resources and opportunities for learning, enhancing skills, and engaging with a vibrant community. As you continue to grow in your Linux journey, you will discover numerous avenues for expanding your knowledge and applying it in diverse environments. From online forums and communities to comprehensive documentation and educational courses, the resources available are plentiful.

One of the most effective ways to deepen your understanding of Linux is by engaging with the Linux community. There are numerous online forums and communities where Linux enthusiasts, ranging from beginners to experts, exchange knowledge, solve problems, and share experiences. Platforms like Reddit's r/linux, LinuxQuestions.org, and Stack Exchange's Unix & Linux section are excellent places to seek help, share insights, and stay updated with the latest developments in the Linux world.

Additionally, mailing lists and IRC (Internet Relay Chat) channels offer real-time communication and support, allowing you to connect with other users and developers. Many Linux distributions have official mailing lists and IRC channels where you can subscribe to discussions or join live chats. These mediums provide an opportunity to engage with developers, contribute to projects, and stay informed about upcoming updates or changes in your preferred distribution.

Comprehensive online documentation is another vital resource for any Linux user. Most Linux distributions and applications maintain official documentation that provides extensive information on installation, configuration, usage, and troubleshooting. Websites like The Linux Documentation Project (TLDP) and Arch Wiki are repositories of detailed guides and how-to articles that cover a wide range of Linux-related topics.

These resources are invaluable for anyone seeking to understand Linux's intricacies and nuances.

Books are also an excellent way to learn about Linux. A wide array of books, ranging from introductory guides for beginners to in-depth explorations of advanced topics, are available for purchase or access at libraries. Titles like "The Linux Command Line" and "Linux Pocket Guide" provide accessible introductions to essential Linux concepts, while more specialized volumes delve into security, networking, and development within the Linux environment.

Online courses and video tutorials offer structured learning experiences, allowing you to gain hands-on experience with Linux systems. Platforms such as Coursera, edX, Udemy, and YouTube host a variety of courses and tutorials tailored to different skill levels, from beginner introductions to advanced administration and development. Engaging with these courses provides an opportunity to reinforce your foundational knowledge and explore more complex aspects of Linux.

Contributing to open-source projects is an effective way to enhance your Linux skills while giving back to the community. Many Linux distributions and applications are open-source, meaning the source code is publicly available, and contributions are welcomed. Participating in these projects allows you to collaborate with experienced developers, learn best practices in software development, and gain insight into how Linux systems and applications are built and maintained.

The importance of networking with professionals and peers in the Linux community cannot be overstated. Attending conferences, workshops, and meetups related to Linux and open-source technology can provide valuable opportunities for learning and connecting with others in the field. Events like Open Source Summit and LinuxCon attract industry experts and offer sessions on a wide range of topics, giving you access to thought leaders and cutting-edge developments in the Linux world.

For those interested in pursuing a career in Linux administration or development, certifications can provide a significant advantage. Certification programs like CompTIA Linux+, Red Hat Certified System Administrator (RHCSA), and Linux Professional Institute Certification (LPIC) validate your expertise and can enhance your employment prospects. Preparing for and completing these certifications demonstrates your commitment to mastering Linux and can open doors to new career opportunities.

Exploring diverse Linux distributions is another way to broaden your understanding of Linux. Each distribution offers unique features, software packages, and community support, catering to different needs and preferences. Experimenting with different distributions can help you discover which suits your requirements best, whether you're interested in running servers, developing software, or simply exploring the versatility of Linux systems.

Staying informed about evolving Linux technologies and innovations is crucial for maintaining an up-to-date understanding of the ecosystem. Subscribing to Linux-related news websites, blogs, and podcasts can keep you informed of emerging trends, new releases, and critical security updates. Following influential figures in the Linux community on social media platforms provides additional insights and perspectives on current developments.

Finally, practice is key to mastering Linux. Setting up personal projects, experimenting with command-line tools, and managing virtual machines or containers provide ongoing learning opportunities. Focusing on real-world scenarios helps develop practical skills and reinforces theoretical knowledge, enabling you to troubleshoot, deploy, and optimize Linux systems confidently.

In summary, the Linux ecosystem offers a wealth of resources and opportunities for exploration and growth. Engaging with community forums, accessing comprehensive documentation, enrolling in educational courses, contributing to open-source projects, networking with peers, and gaining certification are just a few ways to continue building your expertise. By staying curious, committed, and connected, you can fully harness the power of the Linux operating system and enhance your skill set, whether for personal enrichment or professional advancement.